George Hugg

Light in the valley

A new work of great merit for the Sunday school

George Hugg

Light in the valley
A new work of great merit for the Sunday school

ISBN/EAN: 9783337269470

Printed in Europe, USA, Canada, Australia, Japan

Cover: Foto ©Andreas Hilbeck / pixelio.de

More available books at **www.hansebooks.com**

A NEW WORK OF GREAT MERIT

FOR THE

Sunday School, Revivals, Christian Endeavor, Epworth
League, Young People's Society, and all Forward
Movements Along the Line of Battle
for the Master.

BY

GEORGE C. HUGG.

PUBLISHED BY

GEORGE C. HUGG,

2133 NEWKIRK STREET, PHILADELPHIA, PA.

· Preface ·

THE publisher has had so many demands made upon him for a good sacred song book, at a reasonable price, that he has issued LIGHT IN THE VALLEY, to meet the needs of the great body of religious workers in this country. Everything that goes to make up a grand book has been exhausted in the production of this volume, and the price is so reasonable that all may be supplied.

GEO. C. HUGG,
AUTHOR.

LIGHT IN THE VALLEY.

LIGHT IN THE VALLEY.

H. S. L.

H. S. Lowing.

CHORUS.

There's a light............ in the val-ley...... For me, for me;
(3, 4.) There's a light............ in the val-ley...... For you, for you;
There's a light in the valley, For me, for me;

Fine.

There's a light............ in the val-ley...... For me, for me.
There's a light .... in the val-ley...... For you, for you.
There's a light in the valley, For me, for me.

1. O Je- - - sus, come and res - cue Poor me, yes, me;
2. Great char- - - iot of sal - va - tion, Take me, yes, me;
3. O broth- - - er, come to Je - sus, Come now, just now;
4. For Je- - - sus wants to save you Just now, yes, now;
   O Je - sus, come and res- cue, come and res- cue Poor me, yes, me;

D. C.

O Je- - - sus, come and res - cue Poor me, yes, me.
Great char- - - iot of sal - va - tion, Take me, yes, me.
O broth- - - er, come to Je - sus, Come now, just now.
For Je- - - sus wants to save you Just now, yes, now.
O Je - sus, come and res- cue, come and res- cue Poor me, yes, me.

(3)

WALK, MY CHILD, WITH ME.

Rev. Johnson Oatman, Jr.

W. F. Fowler.

1. Once I heard my Saviour speak, "Come, my child, and walk with me;
2. "Through this land of toil and tears, Come, my child, and walk with me;
3. "Through the darkness and the night, Come, my child, and walk with me;

I am strong, but thou art weak, Walk, my child, with me. I will be thy
I will drive a-way thy fears, Walk, my child, with me. Pil-grim to an
I will make thy pathway bright, Walk, my child, with me. When life's clouds have

faith-ful friend; I will thee from harm de-fend; I will guide thee
unknown strand, Would'st thou reach the bet-ter land? Let me lead thee
passed a-way, Thou wilt shine in end-less day; Come, I am the

CHORUS.

to the end; Walk, my child, with me."
by the hand; Walk, my child, with me."   "Walk, my child, with me,
Life, the Way, Walk, my child, with me."

All the way with me; I will safely lead thee home, Walk, my child, with me."

LAUNCH OUT INTO THE DEEP.

Rev. Johnson Oatman, Jr.　　　　　　　　Geo. C. Hugg.

1. All night long the fish - ers sought, But at morn nothing had caught;
2. How these fish- ers were re- paid When the Sav- iour they obeyed!
3. If of grace you would have more, Do not lin - ger near the shore,
4. If you would be sanc - ti - fied, Ho - ly made, in Calv'- ry's tide,
5. Fish- ers would you be, of men? Cut loose ev - 'ry shore line, then;
6. Would you gain that bless - ed shore, There to rest for - ev - er more?

Then they heard the Mas- ter speak, Launch out, launch out in - to the deep.
When they heard the Mas- ter speak, Launch out, launch out in - to the deep.
Lis - ten to the Mas- ter speak, Launch out, launch out in - to the deep.
Lis - ten to the Mas- ter speak, Launch out, launch out in - to the deep.
Lis - ten to the Mas- ter speak, Launch out, launch out in - to the deep.
Lis - ten to the Mas- ter speak, Launch out, launch out in - to the deep.

CHORUS.

No use stay - ing near the shore, Where the bil - lows break and roar;

Lis - ten to the Mas - ter speak, Launch out, launch out in - to the deep.

THERE'S ROOM FOR YOU.

Rev. Johnson Oatman, Jr.

W. F. Fowler.

1. O soul, so far a-way from God, Who long the paths of sin have trod,
2. Although you long on husks have fed, The banquet ta-ble now is spread;
3. You're wanted in the church of God That Christ hath purchased with his blood;
4. And when your cares on earth are past, You'll find a home in heav'n at last;

No lon-ger wander in the cold, The shepherd wants you in his fold.
Here's milk and wine, and hon-ey, too, Come, brother, there is room for you.
'Tis broader far than creed or pew, So, brother, there is room for you.
You'll hear God say, if you are true, "Well done, well done, there's room for you."

CHORUS.

There's room for you, there's room for you, 'Tis not confined to just a few;

God bids you come, his word is true, Come, brother, there is room for you.

JAMES STOCKTON.　　　　　　　　　GEO. C. HUGG.

1. Once the dis-ci-ples wait-ed, Once the dis-ci-ples wait-ed;
2. Then Pe-ter preached a ser-mon, Then Pe-ter preached a ser-mon;
3. Once my poor heart was heav-y, Once my poor heart was heav-y;
4. We had a great re-viv-al, We had a great re-viv-al;
5. It made old Sa-tan trem-ble, It made old Sa-tan trem-ble;
6. I left the world be-hind me, I left the world be-hind me;

'Twas in the up-per cham-ber, When the pow'r came down.
Three thousand were con-vert-ed, When the pow'r came down.
But Je-sus took my bur-den, When the pow'r came down.
And man-y were con-vert-ed, When the pow'r came down.
Be-cause his chain was brok-en, When the pow'r came down.
I start-ed out for glo-ry, When the pow'r came down.

CHORUS.

Like wind, with mighty rushing, Came down the Ho-ly Spir-it;

Oh, there was great re-joic-ing When the pow'r came down.

MY SAVIOUR'S SHELTERING ARMS.

Rev. Johnson Oatman, Jr.   W. F. Fowler.

1. God, in his grace, showed me a place Where life's tempest nev-er more harms;
2. Here I'll a-bide, close to his side, Where the cold world nev-er more charms;
3. Trust in his care; fowls of the air Are fed without storehouse or barns;
4. And when I stand on Jordan's strand, Its wa-ters will cause no a-larms,

I have a sweet, precious retreat In my Saviour's shelter-ing arms.
For here I find sweet peace of mind, In my Saviour's shelter-ing arms.
So there's a store, free ev-er-more, In my Saviour's shelter-ing arms.
For I'll be pressed, close to his breast, In my Saviour's shelter-ing arms.

Chorus.

Here will I rest, close to his breast, Where the tempter nev-er a-larms;

Here I will stay, fold-ed each day In my Saviour's shelter-ing arms.

LET ME LEAN ON THEE.

H. S. L.

H. S. Lowing.

Duet. *With feeling.*

1. Je - sus, at thy cross I bow, Oh, for-give my sins just now;
2. Though I've wandered far a - way, Je - sus bids me come to - day;
3. Let me work and let me sing, Mine own self an off'ring bring;
4. Glo - ry, glo - ry to our King! Let his praise for - ev - er ring;

Lift my bur- dens, make me free, Let me lean, just lean, on thee.
Bring sal - va - tion un - to me; Let me lean, just lean, on thee.
Leaving pleasures, Lord, for thee, Let me lean, just lean, on thee.
And when heaven's gate I see, Let me lean, just lean, on thee.

Chorus.

Lean on thee, lean on thee, Let me lean, just lean, on thee ;
Lean on thee, lean on thee, lean on thee ;

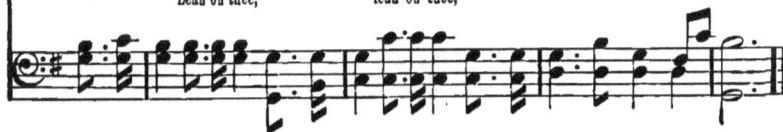

Lean on thee, lean on thee, Let me lean, just lean, on thee.
Lean on thee, lean on thee,

FAIR LIGHTS OF HOME.

JESSE P. TOMPKINS.   GEO. C. HUGG.

1. When we're sail- ing o'er the o - cean, And our ves - sel's nearing home,
2. When we're sail- ing o'er life's o - cean To the port of per- fect peace,
3. When at last we reach the riv - er Where the wa - ters ebb and flow,

We can see the lights that glimmer In the cit - y o'er the foam;
E're we reach the sul - len riv - er, Where our jour- neyings shall cease,
And the Pi - lot, there, is wait- ing, As our barks shall outward go;

Af - ter all the doubt and darkness, When the an - gry bil- lows roar,
Though the clouds may hov - er o'er us, And the storm - y bil- lows roll,
When the mys - tic voyage is o - ver, And the walls ce - les - tial rise,

Oh, how sweet to see the glimmer Of the lights up- on the shore.
There's a light that's ev - er beaming For the guiding of the soul.
How the heav'nly lights will glis- ten, Fair, to our im- mor - tal eyes.

CHORUS.

Oh, lights of home, fair lights of home; Safe in the har-bor, ne'er to roam;
sweet home,   sweet home,

The sails are furled, the anchor cast, Praise God, we're home, safe home, at last.

SWEET THE TIME.

REV. GEORGE BURDER.   W. H. MONK.

1. Sweet the time, ex- ceed- ing sweet! When the saints to- geth - er meet,
2. Sing we then e - ter - nal love, Such as did the Father move:
3. Sing the Son's a - maz- ing love; How he left the realms a - bove,
4. Sing we, too, the Spir- it's love; With our stubborn hearts he strove,

When the Saviour is the theme, When they joy to sing of him.
He beheld the world un - done, Loved the world, and gave his Son.
Took our na- ture and our place, Lived and died to save our race.
Filled our minds with grief and. fear, Brought the precious Saviour near.

MAKE BARE THY MIGHTY ARM.

Rev. Johnson Oatman, Jr.   W. F. Fowler.

1. Lord, help us now to fight, Our ev-'ry fear dis - arm;
2. The foe is press-ing nigh, He would our souls a - larm;
3. We will this bat - tle win, With thee we're safe from harm;
4. Help us our friends to gain, Now held by Sa - tan's charm—

The Lord of hosts will arm the right," Make bare thy might - y arm.
We will not fear if thou art by, Make bare thy might - y arm.
To sweep the bat - tle-field of sin, Make bare thy might - y arm.
To save their souls and break his chain, Make bare thy might - y arm.

Chorus.

O Lord,...... make bare thine arm, Thy might- y, might-y arm;......
    O Lord,   thine arm;

Thy saints are weak, thine aid we seek, Make bare...... thy might - y arm.
                                        Make bare   might - y

GOOD-BYE.

(PARTING HYMN.)

Rev. Johnson Oatman, Jr. **Geo. C. Hugg.**

13

1. These scenes, so bright, now take their flight As birds in summer seem to fly;
2. As oft we meet, and dear ones greet, Heart speaks to heart and eye to eye;
3. Sometime we'll meet, sometime we'll greet Each other in that land on high;

A- gain we stand with parting hand, Good-bye, good-bye, good - bye.
Time speeds a- way, and soon we say, Good-bye, good-bye, good - bye.
There we will stay, and nev - er say, Good-bye, good-bye, good - bye.

CHORUS.

Good-bye, good-bye, we breathe a sigh, We say farewell with tear-dimmed eye;

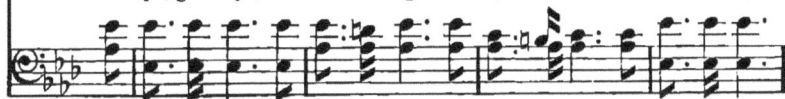

God bless you all, God keep you all, Good-bye, good-bye, good - bye.

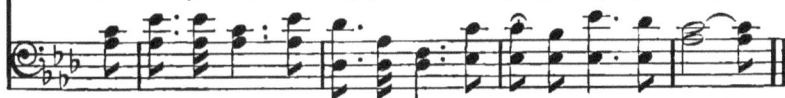

THERE SHALL BE NO MORE SEA.

Rev. Alson M. Doak.   (Rev. 21 : 1.)   Thos. S. Evans.

Andante moderato.

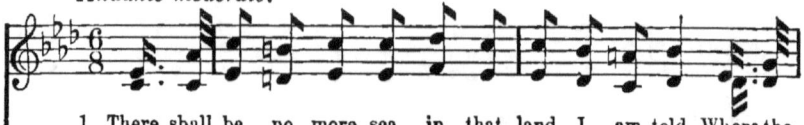

1. There shall be no more sea in that land, I am told, Where the
2. He shall tell me the rea - son he carried a - way That sweet
3. Oh, I won- der, sometimes, why God takes from my heart Those dear

cres.

walls are of jas- per and streets are of gold ; Yet, as o'er the wild waves of life's
an- gel whose smile added light to the day—The pure child that went out from the
friends from whose love 'tis heart-crushing to part ; But he speaks through the storm: "Trust and

cres.

rit.

con- flict I'm tossed, I still wonder, sometimes, if my soul shall be lost.
reach of earth's wrong, Lured a- way by the mu- sic of heav- en - ly song.
soon you shall see That I've called them to do nobler ser- vice for me."

rit.

Solo. *Andante.*

But although there are mys - ter - ies dark and unknown, I am
And that mother, who went from her la - bor a - way, When her
Yes, life here has its con- flicts and mys - ter - ies deep, And the

Duet.
rit.   *a tempo.*

sure, in their midst I shall not be a- lone, For that One who on earth lived a
hair, by the weight of earth's crosses grew gray, I shall find in that land sweet with
sorrows of life make the heart often weep ; But when all have rolled by, in that

rit.   *a tempo.*

life without stain, Shall be close to my side to make ev - 'ry-thing plain.
flow'rs from life's tree, Tho' now hidden from view by death's cold, cru- el sea.
land I shall be, Where in raptures of joy I shall known no more sea.

Volti subito.

CHORUS.

I shall stand in the storm but a little while, For the Master has said to me

That I soon shall be tasting the pleasures sweet Of that land where there is no sea.

no sea.

DEPTH OF MERCY!—CAN THERE BE.

REV. CHARLES WESLEY.   Arr. fr. VON WEBER.

1. Depth of mer- cy!—can there be   Mer- cy still reserved for me?
2. I have long withstood his grace; Long provoked him to his face:
3. Kindled his re-lent-ings are;   Me he now de-lights to spare;
4. There for me the Sav-iour stands; Shows his wounds and spreads his hands!

Can my God his wrath for-bear? Me, the chief of sinners, spare?
Would not hearken to his calls; Grieved him by a thousand falls.
Cries, How shall I give thee up?—Lets the lift-ed thunder drop.
God is love! I know, I feel: Je-sus weeps, and loves me still.

JUST ONE TOUCH.

BIRDIE BELL.   J. HOWARD ENTWISLE.

SOLO. *Slow, with expression.*

1. Just one touch as he moves a-long, Pushed and pressed by the jostling throng,
2. Just one touch and he makes me whole, Speaks sweet peace to my sin-sick soul
3. Just one touch! and the work is done, I am saved by the blessed Son,
4. Just one touch! and he turns to me, O the love in his eyes I see!
5. Just one touch! by his mighty pow'r, He can heal thee this ver-y hour,

Just one touch, and the weak was strong, Cured by the Healer di - vine.
At his feet all my burdens roll, Cured by the Healer di - vine.
I will sing while the a-ges run, Cured by the Healer di - vine.
I am his for he hears my plea, Cured by the Healer di - vine.
Thou cans't hear tho' the tempests low'r, Cured by the Healer di - vine.

CHORUS.

Just one touch as he passes by, He will list to the faintest cry,

Come and be saved while the Lord is nigh, Christ is the Healer di-vine.
divine.

GIVE US THE BATTLE.

IDA L. REED.   W. F. FOWLER.

1. Give us the battle, Lord Je - ho - vah, Strongly the foes beset us 'round;
2. Give us the battle, lead us on - ward. Help us to triumph o- ver sin;
3. Give us the battle, we are read - y Onward to move at thy com- mand;
4. Give us the battle, Lord Je - ho - vah, Strengthen thy legions for the fight;

Strengthen our hearts for the con - flict, Let thy sustain - ing grace abound.
Self, thro' thy love, may we con - quer, Keep thou our frail hearts pure within.
On thy sure promises re - ly - ing, Firm- ly for thee, dear Lord, we stand.
Strong are the foes that be - set us, Give us thy grace and ho - ly might.

CHORUS.
UNISON.   PARTS.   UNISON.   PARTS.

Give us the battle, Lord Je- ho- vah, Lead us to vic- to- ry in thy name;

Give us the battle, Lord Je - hovah, Wilt thou thy might and thy pow'r proclaim?

AT THE EVENTIDE.

Rev. Johnson Oatman, Jr.

Geo. C. Hugg.

1. O'er the ocean's foam is a land ahead, Where the white-robed throng with their
2. Oft I meet with foes who would turn me back, With the chains of sin, and the
3. We have toil and care all a- long the way, For the waves are rough, and the
4. There the loved and lost of the years gone by, Sing the new, new song by their

Lord a - bide; For that peaceful shore all my sails are spread, I will
snares of pride; They will fol - low me all a- long life's track, But I'll
o- cean wide; But our trials will cease, at the close of day, When we
Saviour's side; But we'll part no more, while the a - ges fly, When we

Chorus.

reach that land at the e - ven- tide.
lose them all at the e - ven- tide.
find sweet rest at the e - ven- tide.
gath - er home at the e - ven- tide.

Yes, my sails are spread for the

glo - ry - land; I shall all the storms of this life out- ride; When I

reach that port on the golden strand, I will anchor there at the e - ventide.

PRECIOUS BLOOD.

Miss Frances Havergal.

A. H. A.

1. Precious, pre-cious blood of Je-sus, Shed on Cal-va-ry;
2. Tho' thy sins are red like crimson, Deep in scar-let glow,
3. Precious blood that hath redeemed us! All the price is paid!
4. Precious blood, by this we conquer; In the fierc-est fight

Shed for reb-els, shed for sin-ners, Shed for thee!
Je-sus' pre-cious blood shall wash thee White as snow.
Per-fect par-don now is of-fered, Peace is made.
Sin and Sa-tan o-ver-com-ing, By its might.

Refrain.

Precious blood, cleansing flood, Washing the sins of the world a-way;

Precious blood, fountain free, Flowing for sinners like you and me.

OVER IN THE GOLDEN LAND.

Rev. Johnson Oatman, Jr. Geo. C. Hugg.

Solo. **Semi-Chorus.**

1. We are marching forth to a home on high, O-ver in the golden land;
2. We shall meet our loved ones up-on that shore, O-ver in the golden land;
3. Je-sus Christ will give us a crown at last, O-ver in the golden land;
4. We will sing the songs that the ransomed sing, O-ver in the golden land;

Solo. **Semi-Chorus.**

We shall gather there in the by and by, O-ver in the golden land.
With the vict'ry won, and the bat-tle o'er, O-ver in the golden land.
When our cares and tri-als are from us cast, O-ver in the golden land.
Thro' the endless years will the mu-sic ring, O-ver in the golden land.

Full Chorus.

O-ver in the golden land, O-ver in the gold-en land;
golden land, golden land;

With our tri-als past, we shall meet at last, O-ver in the golden land.

REV. JOHNSON OATMAN, JR.   W. F. FOWLER.

Boldly.

1. We look around on ev-'ry side, The seeds of sin are scattered wide;
2. We must by faith to Christ draw near, But we must work while we are here;
3. We do not have for work to pray, Our work will come to us each day;
4. Then work for God, O do your best, In heav'n at last you then can rest;

There's work for you in ev-'ry land, While he is calling, lend a hand.
We are not called to i - dly stand, The Lord wants workers, lend a hand.
Your work and mine the Lord has planned, None else can do it, lend a hand.
But till you reach that better land, There's work for Je-sus, lend a hand.

CHORUS.

O............ lend a hand,........ yes,......... lend a hand,.......
O lend a hand,   O lend a hand, yes, lend a hand,   yes, lend a hand,

The......... Master's work........ is............ great and grand; ....
The Master's work   is great and grand, The Master's work   is great and grand;

Go,.......... work to - day,..... .... at............ his com - mand,......
Go, work to-day, at his command, Go, work to-day, at his command,

While....... he yet calls......... us, O lend............ a hand.,.......
While he yet calls, O lend a hand, While he yet calls, O lend a hand.

JESUS! NAME OF WONDROUS LOVE!

Rev. William W. How, D. D.   R. Redhead.

1. Je - sus ! name of wondrous love ! Name all oth - er names a - bove !
2. Je - sus ! name de-creed of old : To the maid - en moth-er told,
3. Je - sus ! name of priceless worth To the fall - en sons of earth,
4. Je - sus ! name of wondrous love ! Hu- man name of God a - bove ;

Un - to which must ev - 'ry knee Bow in deep hu - mil - i - ty.
Kneeling in her low - ly cell, By the an - gel Ga - bri - el.
For the prom- ise that it gave—"Je - sus shall his peo - ple save."
Pleading on - ly this, we flee, Helpless, O our God to thee.

REV. JOHNSON OATMAN, JR.   REV. W. J. STUART, A. M.

Feelingly.

1. O   blessed Saviour, be my guide, And keep me   ev - er near thy side;
2. Tho' skies may be   as dark as night, I'll trust in thee, my Lord, my light;
3. Tho' for- tune frowns tho' rich-es   fly, Tho' friends with cold- ness pass me by,
4. And when I reach my journey's end, I'll trust in thee, my dearest Friend;

For this   I know, where'er it   be,   I can with safe - ty fol - low thee.
For at   thy voice the shadows flee, And I with joy will fol - low thee.
Then, knowing thou art true to me, My all in all, I'll fol - low thee.
I'll hear thee say - ing, "Come with me," Then I will glad - ly fol - low thee.

CHORUS.

I'll fol - low thee, I'll fol - low thee, No mat- ter where thou leadest me;

Thro' time and thro' e - ter - ni - ty, My Saviour, I   will fol - low thee.

THE GOOD OLD WAY.

B. H. WINSLOW.   ALLEN L. WINSLOW.

With spirit.

1. We are go - ing forth on a jour - ney long, But we cheer our
2. We shall meet with sin on our jour - ney home, We shall feel the
3. When the jour- ney ends at the shin - ing strand, And our eyes shall

way with a pil- grim song; "With our Father's hand leading night and day,
waves of af- flic- tion come ; But our lov- ing Guide will our strength re- new,
look on that far off land ; How our hearts will thrill as with joy we say,

REFRAIN.

We are go - ing home in the Good Old Way."
And will walk with us all our journey thro'. ⎬ 'Tis our Father's way, by the
"What a bless- ed path was that Good Old Way."

prophets trod ; 'Tis a joy - ful way, and it leads us un - to God; "With our

rit.

Father's hand leading night and day, We are go- ing home in the Good Old Way.

I LIVE BY THE RIVER OF PEACE.

Rev. Johnson Oatman, Jr.   Geo. C. Hugg.

With expression.

1. Man - y long years I sailed o'er life's o - cean, On its waves I was
2. Let the great, bus - y world swing a- round me, But no more do I
3. I do not live a - lone by the riv - er, For the arm - y of

tossed to and fro; Then my life was a constant com- mo- tion,
dread its a - larms; For secure, since my Saviour has found me,
God dwelleth there, And the Lord God of hosts will de - liv - er

And for rest I had nowhere to go; Then I heard a sweet
I am safe ev - er more in his arms; For he came when sin's
From all foes that my feet would en - snare. All my trust in the

voice gen - tly saying, "Come to me, all life's tumult will cease;" Now no
fet - ters did bind me, And he gave to my soul sweet re - lease; Now the
Lord I'm re - pos- ing, And I find that my joys here increase; And I'll

rit.

more on the waves I am straying, But I live by the riv-er of peace.
world and its cares are behind me, For I live by the riv-er of peace.
live with my Lord, at life's closing, If I live by the riv-er of peace.

I COME TO THEE.

EMMA A. TIFFANY.
GEO. C. HUGG.

With feeling.

1. Je - sus, dear, I come to thee, Thou a- lone canst make me free ;
2. Je - sus, dear, to thee I bring All of earth to which I cling ;
3. Je - sus, dear, I come to thee, Wilt thou all my ref - uge be,

Thou a - lone canst cleanse from sin. Make me pure with - out, with- in :
All the friends my heart holds dear To thy al - tar now bring near ;
Thro' the thorn- y maze of life, Thro' the ba - ttles, thro' its strife ;

Wounded, at thy feet I lie, Do not, do not pass me by.
Keep them safe with- in thy fold, Grant them rest and joy un- told.
When the fi - nal hour doth come, Wilt thou guide me safe - ly home ?

W. S.

WM. STONE.

1. Now I hear my Saviour call - ing, There's a spe- cial work for me;
2. What a joy to work for Je - sus, Tho' in weakness it may be;
3. Send me where thou chooseth, Sav-iour, I am will-ing to o - bey;
4. Here's my life, O lov - ing Sav - iour, Not an hour will I withhold;

Give to me thy choicest bless-ing, All of self I give to thee.
Just a lit - tle thing, how precious, Yet he did so much for me.
On - ly let me feel thy presence, Walk be-side me day by day.
Fill my soul with grace o'erflow-ing, Truth and light to me un- fold.

CHORUS.

Je- sus is call-ing, call- ing to me, O what a joy to work for thee;

Je- sus is call-ing, call- ing to me, Lord, I'll glad - ly work for thee.

Harriet E. Jones. J. Howard Entwisle.

1. Will you come to the feast? Will you sup with the Lord? He will welcome the least
2. Will you come and be fed By our Saviour and Lord? With our great King and head
3. O- pen wide is the door To the banqueting hall — Are you hungry and poor?

To his boun - ti-ful board; There's enough and to spare, and right roy- al the fare,
Will you sit at the board? He invites you to-day, dare you longer de- lay?
There is food for you all ; Come and sup with the King, with our Prophet and Priest,

CHORUS.

Will you come, one and all, to the feast? } Will you come, will you come,......
Is there one who will dare to say nay? } Will you come, will you come,
Come, oh, come, one and all, to the feast? }

Will you come to the feast? For the world there is room, Lo! the King will pre-

side, for each guest will provide, Will you come, will you come to the feast?

WHEN THE ROLL IS CALLED.

"Another book was opened, which is the Book of life."—Rev. 20: 12.

Rev. W. G. C.

Rev. W. G. Cooper.

1. When shall close the earth's long a- ges, Christ shall come to claim his own;
2. When the "Book of Life" is opened, and the crown of glo - ry giv'n
3. When the ar- mies of Je - ho- vah shout "the bat- tles all are o'er!"
4. Let us then be ev - er faithful 'till the Mas- ter bid us rise,

And he shall in glo - rious maj - es - ty ap - pear. When earth's
To the saved of earth, im - mor - tal, bright and fair! When with
And their "wel- come home" and glad re - un - ion share; When in
And shall close our life of la - bor, toil and care; Then we'll

teeming millions gath - er up be- fore the judgment throne; And the
vic - to - ry they gath - er for their joy - ous rest in hear'n, When the
grand review they're mustered out up - on the oth - er shore, And the
sweet- ly rest with Je - sus in our home be - yond the skies, When the

FINE. CHORUS.

roll is called up yonder, I'll be there. When the roll........ is called up
roll is called up yonder, I'll be there.
roll is called up yonder, I'll be there.
roll is called up yonder, We'll be there.

When the roll

5 Spirit guiding us aright,
Spirit making darkness light,
Spirit of resistless might;
Hear us, Holy Spirit.

6 Thou, whom Jesus from his throne
Gave to cheer and help his own,
That they might not be alone;
Hear us, Holy Spirit.

7 Thou by whom our souls are fed
With the true and living bread,
Even him who for us bled;
Hear us, Holy Spirit.

8 Come to raise us when we fall,
And, when snares our souls enthrall,
Lead us back with gentle call;
Hear us, Holy Spirit.

9 Keep us in the narrow way,
Warn us when we go astray,
Plead within us when we pray;
Hear us, Holy Spirit.

10 Holy, loving, as thou art,
Come, and live within our heart,
Never from us to depart;
Hear us, Holy Spirit.

32 "WEEP NOT FOR ME."

Rev. Johnson Oatman, Jr. (Luke 23 : 28.) W. F. Fowler.

Andante.

pp

Weep not for me,.............. weep not for me, for me.
Weep not for me, weep not for me.

Sostenuto.

1. Tho' o'er my life-less form you may be bend - ing, For now my song with
2. But think of me as on - ly gone be - fore you; From heav'nly heights I
3. Tho' now with grief your heart is sad and ach - ing, Tho' now with sobs your
4. Tho' now you feel a sense of des - o - la - tion, For those who mourn there
5. Tho' 'tis God's will that earthly ties should sev - er, We'll meet again, where

an - gel notes is blend - ing; I'm safe at home, where joys are nev - er
will be watching o'er you, Just by the gates I will be wait- ing
bo- som may be shak - ing; Mine eyes have seen the gold- en morning
is a con - so - la - tion; In heav'n a - bove will come no sep - a -
part- ing com- eth nev - er; There, hand in hand, we'll live and love for

CHORUS.

end - ing, Weep not for me. Dear friends, weep not for me, but still your
for you, Weep not for me.
break - ing, Weep not for me.
ra - tion, Weep not for me.
ev - er, Weep not for me.

Weep not, but still your

sor - row, Dear friends, weep not for me, but com - fort bor - row; In
Weep not,

heav'n a - bove we'll meet a - gain to - mor - row, Weep not for me.

OUR BLEST REDEEMER, ERE HE BREATHED.

Harriet Auber.   J. B. Dykes.

1. Our blest Redeem - er, ere he breathed His ten - der, last farewell,
2. He came, sweet influence to im - part, A gracious, will - ing Guest,
3. And ev - 'ry vir - tue we pos-sess, And ev - 'ry vic - t'ry won,
4. Spir - it of pur - i - ty and grace! Our weakness pity - ing see;

A Guide, a Com - fort - er bequeathed, With us to dwell.
While he can find one hum - ble heart Where - in to rest.
And ev - 'ry thought of ho - li - ness Is his a - - lone.
Oh, make our hearts thy dwell - ing place, And worth - ier thee!

34 EVERY BRIDGE IS BURNED BEHIND ME.

REV. JOHNSON OATMAN, JR.   GEO. C. HUGG.

1. Since I start-ed out to find thee, Since I to the Ark did flee,
2. Thou didst hear my plea so kind-ly, Thou didst grant me so much grace;
3. Cares of life per-plex and grind me, Yet I keep the nar-row way;
4. All in all, I ev-er find thee, Saviour, Lov-er, Brother, Friend;

Ev-'ry bridge is burned behind me, I will nev-er turn from thee.
Ev-'ry bridge is burned behind me, I will ne'er my steps retrace.
Ev-'ry bridge is burned behind me, I from thee will nev-er stray.
Ev-'ry bridge is burned behind me, I will serve thee to the end.

CHORUS.

Strengthen all the ties that bind me Clos-er, clos-er, Lord, to thee;

Ev-'ry bridge is burned behind me, Thine I ev-er-more will be.

Rev. Johnson Oatman, Jr.   W. F. Fowler.

1. The sinner's friend is our Saviour dear, His on - ly hope and plea;
2. O where on earth can we find a friend So faithful and so true?
3. To friends of earth we must say good-by, When death comes to our door;

Tho' the world forsakes, he will still be near, The same evermore is he.
Who will pi - lot us to our journey's end, And guide us the whole way through?
But we'll go with him to that home on high, And live on that peaceful shore.

CHORUS.

There nev - er, no, nev - er, was such a friend, We'll

ev - er, yes, ev - er, on him de - pend; For ev - er and

ev - er, when we as - cend, We'll praise our Sav - iour and King.

WE ARE ABLE TO GO UP AND POSSESS THE LAND.

(Numbers 13: 30.)

Rev. Johnson Oatman, Jr.   Geo. C. Hugg.

1. We are on our way to Canaan, and we'll reach it by and by,
2. This is called the land of promise, for 'twas promised by the Lord
3. In that blessed, blessed country there's a home for ev - 'ry one
4. We will have to cross the riv - er when we reach the bor- der-land,

Tho' to keep us from that country all our en - e -mies may try;
That some day the wea - ry ex - iles to their homes should be restored;
Who will fol- low our Command- er till the set - ting of the sun,
But we will not fear the current tho' our feet with - in it stand;

But no mat - ter who op - pose, We will con- quer all our foes;
So be - liev -ing in his Word, And re - ly - ing on his sword,
And where Je - sus goes a - head We will nev - er fear to tread;
For the wa - ters will give way, And we'll find, at close of day,

We are a - ble to go up and pos - sess the land.

Chorus.

We are a- - - - - - - ble to go up,
We are a - ble to go up and pos - sess the land,

We are a- - - - - - - ble to go up;
We are a - ble to go up and pos - sess the land;

With our King to go be - fore us, And his ban - ner float - ing

o'er us, We are a - ble to go up and pos - sess the land.

I KNOW THAT MY REDEEMER LIVES.

WILLIAM RHODA.   H. S. LOWING.

1. I know that my Re-deem-er lives, For he hath made me   free ;
2. I know that my Re-deem-er lives, 'Twas he who made me   whole ;
3. I know that my Re-deem-er lives, Thank God, he lives to - day !
4. I know that my Re-deem-er lives In mansions bright and   fair ;

He made my stubborn heart re-joice, And now the light I   see.
He turned my darkness   in - to light, And saved my trembling   soul.
He lives to make his   peo- ple free, Oh, why will you de - lay ?
And when the hour of death shall come, I know I'll meet him   there.

CHORUS.

Hal - le - lu - jah, Je - sus saves me, Glo - ry, glo - ry   to his name !

Vic - to - ry   is   on my ban - ner, I will now   his love proclaim.

A FULL SURRENDER.

REV. JOHNSON OATMAN, JR.

GEO. C. HUGG.

1. A full sur-ren-der I have made, I've giv-en all to Je-sus;
2. My hands, my feet, my head, my heart, I've giv-en all to Je-sus;
3. My loss or gain, my hopes and fears, I've giv-en all to Je-sus;
4. My mon-ey, la-bors, burdens, cares, I've giv-en all to Je-sus;
5. My life, my love, my fam-i-ly, I've giv-en all to Je-sus;

My all is on the al-tar laid, I've giv-en all to Je-sus.
I've not retained a sin-gle part, I've giv-en all to Je-sus.
My health and strength, my grief and tears, I've giv-en all to Je-sus.
My voice, my pen, my songs, my prayers, I've giv-en all to Je-sus.
For time, and for e-ter-ni-ty, I've giv-en all to Je-sus.

CHORUS.

I've surrendered all, I've surrendered all;
surrendered all, surrendered all;

Ev-'ry-thing is on the al-tar, I've surrendered all..............
surrendered all.

THE SUNDAY SCHOOL ARMY.

Rev. Johnson Oatman, Jr.   W. F. Fowler.

Tempo di Marcia.

1. See our might-y arm-y, as we march a-long, We are
2. Bands of hap-py chil-dren, marching ev-'ry day, We are
3. As we march, we're giv-ing prais-es to our King, We are
4. As we march, we car-ry neith-er gun nor sword, We are

marching on to vic-to-ry; Ne'er be-fore were soldiers half so
marching on to vic-to-ry; We will win the bat-tle, if we
marching on to vic-to-ry; Lis-ten to our voic-es, how we
marching on to vic-to-ry; We will get to heav-en, trusting

bold and strong, We are marching on to vic-to-ry.
watch and pray, We are marching on to vic-to-ry.
shout and sing, We are marching on to vic-to-ry.
in the Lord, We are marching on to vic-to-ry.

CHORUS.
Unison.

Vic-to-ry, vic-to-ry. *Organ.*   We

are an arm-y with ban-ners, Ban-ners, ban-ners, We

Parts.

are an arm-y with ban-ners, We're marching up to God.

SWEET IS THE WORK, O LORD.

MISS HARRIET AUBER.   J. BARNBY.

1. Sweet is the work, O Lord,	Thy glorious name to sing;
2. Sweet—at the dawn-ing light,	Thy boundless love to tell;
3. Sweet—on this day of rest,	To join in heart and voice,
4. To songs of praise and joy	Be ev-'ry Sab-bath given,

To praise and pray—to hear thy word, And grateful off'rings bring.
And when approach the shades of night, Still on the theme to dwell.
With those who love and serve thee best, And in thy name re-joice.
That such may be our blest employ E-ter-nal-ly in heaven.

THE SHADOW OF THE CROSS.

Rev. Johnson Oatman.

Geo. C. Hugg.

With expression.

1. O'er the sunlight falls a shadow, Where life's breakers foam and toss;
2. Yes, the shad- ow fall-eth ev - er, Un- de- filed by earth- ly dross;
3. While it breathes of hope and mer- cy, May it nev - er suf- fer loss;
4. When at last my feet are standing Where the Jordan's bil- lows toss.

Falling o - ver earth and heaven, Blessed shad - ow of the cross.
Falling o - ver saint and sinner, Blessed shad - ow of the cross.
In its shade we love to lin- ger, Blessed shad - ow of the cross.
Let me die beneath that shadow, Blessed shad - ow of the cross,

Chorus.

f   *m*

Wonderful shadow, heaven- ly shadow, Angels ne'er thy shade can gloss;

f   *m*

Ra - di- ant shadow, beau- ti- ful shadow, Hallowed shadow of the cross.

GRANVILLE JONES.   E. M. DOUTHIT.

1. Wea - ry hands will cease from la - bor, Fold - ed, they at rest will lie,
2. Sor- row will not last for - ev - er, Tears not al - ways dim the eye;
3. Pain is not our last- ing por - tion, Balm descend - eth from on high,
4. Death is not to be e - ter - nal, Tho' we all are doomed to die;

For we have a bur-den bear - er, And his com - ing draweth nigh.
Je - sus is our con - so - la - tion, And his com - ing draweth nigh.
For we have a great Phy - si - cian, And his com - ing draweth nigh.
Je - sus is the res - ur - rec - tion, And his com - ing draweth nigh.

CHORUS.

Yes, the wea - ry night is pass - ing, Dawn is break - ing in the sky;

We shall hail the glad to- mor- row, For his com - ing draweth nigh.

44 SPREADING THE HEAVENLY SUNSHINE.

Rev. Johnson Oatman, Jr.   Geo. C. Hugg.

1. This is my mission, wherev- er I go, Spreading the heaven- ly sunshine;
2. Je- sus hath sent me to glean by the way, Spreading the heaven- ly sunshine;
3. Hearts bend to Je- sus as flow'rs to the sun, Spreading the heaven- ly sunshine;
4. Burdens are lightened as I move a- long, Spreading the heaven- ly sunshine;
5. Then let me work till life's la-bors shall close, Spreading the heaven- ly sunshine;

O- ver life's pathway of sor-row and woe, Spreading the sunshine of love.
So I am working by night and by day, Spreading the sunshine of love.
While man- y souls for the Master are won, Spreading the sunshine of love.
Sadness is banished by mu- sic and song, Spreading the sunshine of love.
Then let me sink in death's qui- et re- pose, Spreading the sunshine of love.

Chorus.

Spreading the light of the Gospel of God, Spreading the heaven- ly sunshine;

O- ver some one who in sorrow may plod, Spreading the heavenly sunshine.

LOOK ALONG THE SHORE.

"And Jesus said unto them, Come ye after me, and I will make you to become fishers of men."—Mark 1: 17.

A. F. M.   A. F. MYERS.

1. On sin's bar - ren, rock - y coast, Life-barks per - ish o'er and o'er,
2. In the darkness of the night, 'Mid the an - gry breakers' roar,
3. Hum- ble tasks are left undone For the work that's hon- ored more ;
4. Lured by Sa - tan's pow'r combined, Lives are shipwrecked by the score ;

Precious souls are oft - en lost, Brother, look a - long the shore.
Some poor soul may ask for light, Brother, look a - long the shore.
Seek some poor, ne-glect - ed one, Brother, look a - long the shore.
Go, then, quick-ly, and you'll find Souls to save a - long the shore.

CHORUS.

Look a - long the shore, my brother,' Look a-long the shore ;

Quick - ly go, and you may rescue Precious souls a - long the shore.

By permission of A. F. Myers. owner of copyright.

CROWN HIS HEAD.

SELECTED.

A. H. A.

1. Crown his head with endless bless - ing, Who in God the Father's name,
2. Lo, Je - ho - vah, we a - dore thee—Thee, our Saviour; thee, our God!
3. Je - sus, thee our Saviour hail - ing, Thee, our God in praise we own;
4. Now ye saints his pow'r con - fess - ing, In your grateful strains a - dore;

With compassion nev - er ceas - ing, Came sal - va - tion to proclaim.
From that throne the beams of glo - ry Shine thro' all the world a - broad.
Highest hon - ors, nev - er fail - ing, Rise e - ter - nal 'round thy throne.
For his mer - cy, nev - er ceas - ing, Flows and flows for ev - er - more.

CHORUS.

Crown, his head,...... the Lord of glo - ry, Crown his head,...... the King of
Crown his head,   Crown his head,

kings; Lo, he comes,...... to earth de - scend - ing, Life and
king of kings;   Lo, he comes,

health to all he brings. Crown his head,...... crown his head with endless blessing.
                        Crown his head,

Rev. Johnson Oatman, Jr. Rev. W. J. Stuart, A. M.

1. Come, brother, let us hear you tell If with your spir-it it is well;
2. Come, let us hear you tell once more Of how you found the o-pen door,
3. Come, tell if all a-long the way You find it light from day to day;

Is your heart filled with heav'nly love? Is your name written up a-bove?
And heard the bless-ed Saviour say, "Come in, I am the Life, the Way."
Does Je-sus lead by waters still? Does he with joy your bo-som thrill?

Then, brother, raise on joy-ful wing The praises of your Saviour, King,
Come, tell of how the light shone in, When first you lost your load of sin,
Then tell it out, and ev-er sing The praises of your God and King,

And tell to wit-ness-es around, If peace and par-don you have found.
And felt your feet on sol-id ground, Your burden lost, your Saviour found.
Un-til with him, a-bove the sky, You'll sing his praise, while a-ges fly.

JESUS, NOW I COME TO THEE.

Rev. W. W. Hall.   Thos. S. Evans.

1. Je - sus, now I come to thee, Cleanse my heart and set me free;
2. Je - sus, now thou art my Friend, And on me rich blessing send;
3. Bless- ed Je - sus, keep me white, In the darkness of the night;
4. I'm a sin - ner saved by grace; In thy sa - cred, heav'nly place,

Con - secrate me now to thee, Thy child for - ev - er - more.
Thou canst keep me, to the end, Thy child for - ev - er - more.
Al- ways walk- ing in the light, Thy child for - ev - er - more.
I shall see him face to face, His child for - ev - er - more.

CHORUS.

Je - sus, Sav- iour, pi - lot me O - ver life's tem- pestuous sea;

From this day, oh, let me be Thy child for - ev - er - more.

Rev. Johnson Oatman, Jr.   W. F. Fowler.

1. There's a place for ev-'ry one, In the path of du - ty;
2. 'Tis a bless - ed place to be, In the path of du - ty;
3. Help to oth - ers we can give, In the path of du - ty;
4. O 'tis sweet with Christ to walk, In the path of du - ty;
5. Cares of life are left be - hind, In the path of du - ty;

There is work that must be done, In the path of du - ty.
Je - sus comes and walks with me, In the path of du - ty.
Souls once dead are made to live; In the path of du - ty.
O 'tis good with him to talk, In the path of du - ty.
Heaven's gate I soon shall find, In the path of du - ty.

CHORUS.

In the path of du - ty, Bless - ed path of du - ty;

Joy un-speak - a - ble I find, In the path of du - ty.

BRIGHTER EVERY DAY.

Rev. Johnson Oatman, Jr.   Geo. C. Hugg.

1. O my broth-er, have you started for the heavenly land? Don't you
2. As you la-bor in the vineyard for the Mas-ter here, Don't you
3. When your spir-it feels the breezes from the oth'-er shore, Don't you
4. Ver-y soon you'll cross the riv-er to the gold-en land, Don't you

find the path grows brighter ev-'ry day? Are you guided on the
find the path grows brighter ev-'ry day? As you hear him sweetly
find the path grows brighter ev-'ry day? When you see your dear ones
find the path grows brighter ev-'ry day? Ver-y soon you'll live and

ev-'ry day?

journey by the Sav-iour's hand? Don't you find the path grows brighter ev-'ry day?
whisper words of hope and cheer, Don't you find the path grows brighter ev-'ry day?
leave you to return no more, Don't you find the path grows brighter ev-'ry day?
mingle with that blood-washed band, Don't you find the path grows brighter ev-'ry day?

As you praise his name with a ho-ly song, As you linger in his courts to
As you tell the world of a Saviour's love, As you point men to the nar-row
For they're hap-py now in that home on high, All their trials and tears have passed a-
Where the Lamb of God is the cit-y's light, Where night has for-ev-er passed a-

pray,   As you firm - ly stand   in the fight against the wrong, Don't you
way,   As you help some soul   on toward that home a- bove, Don't you
way ;   As they watch your course in the journey to the sky, Don't you
way,   And the roadway fair   is the blessed path of right, Don't you
courts to pray,

find the path grows brighter ev -'ry day ? Don't you find....... .... the path grows
Don't you find

CHORUS.

brighter   ev - 'ry   day? Don't you   see............   the light   ce-
Don't you see

les - tial   on   the way; All the time that you have striven On the

upward road to ˙heaven, Don't you find the path grows brighter ev - 'ry day?

HE'S EVERYTHING TO ME.

Rev. Johnson Oatman, Jr.

Geo. C. Hugg.

Trustingly.

1. I have a song I love to sing; Since Jesus 'set me free,
2. He broke the chains that compassed me, When I to him did flee,
3. He nev - er will for - sake me here, Tho' oth - er friends should flee;
4. I'll sing his prais - es all thro' time And thro' e - ter - ni - ty;

And led me to the liv - ing spring, He's ev - 'ry-thing to me.
And since he gave me lib - er - ty, He's ev - 'ry-thing to me.
With faith in Christ, I will not fear, He's ev - 'ry-thing to me.
I still will praise my Lord di - vine, He's ev - 'ry-thing to me.

CHORUS.

O sing the praise of Je - sus, sing, Blest Lamb of Cal - va - ry;

My love, my life, my Lord, my King, He's ev - 'ry-thing to me.

REV. JOHNSON OATMAN, JR. REV. W. J. STEWART, A. M.

Cheerfully.

1. Learning ev - 'ry day, words of truth and grace, At the feet of Christ,
2. Learning ev - 'ry day of the will of God, Learning how to pass
3. Learning ev - 'ry day as a lit - tle child, Learning how to live
4. Learning how to live in a world of sin, Learning how to have

what a bless - ed place; List'ning to his voice, look - ing in his face,
'neath the chast'ning rod; Learning how to tread where the saints have trod,
pa - tient, kind and mild; Learning how to live pure and un - de - filed,
joy and peace with - in; Learning how to have heav - en here be - gun,

CHORUS.

Sit - ting at the feet of Je - sus. Learning ev - 'ry day,

all a - bout the way, Learning how to watch, learning how to pray;

Learning how to live, learning how to · die, Sit - ting at the feet of Je - sus.

G. C. H.   GEO. C. HUGG.

1. When the ransomed shall re-turn to Zi-on fair,   When they
2. When I hear their songs, and view the sheaves they bear,   When they
3. When they go up home, e-ter-nal life to share,   When they

Zi-on fair,

cross the riv-er Jordan I'll be there;   In their songs and ev-er-
cross the riv-er Jordan I'll be there;   Oh, what rapture! oh, what
cross the riv-er Jordan I'll be there;   There we'll sing the song of

I'll be there;

lasting joy I'll share,   At the crossing of the Jordan I'll be there.
bliss beyond compare!   At the crossing of the Jordan I'll be there.
"Mo-ses and the Lamb,"   At the crossing of the Jordan I'll be there.

joy I'll share,   I'll be there.

CHORUS.

I'll be there,............ I'll be there,   At the crossing of the
At the crossing, at the crossing of the Jordan I'll be there,

Jor-dan I'll be there ; In the morn,............. bright and
I'll be there; In the morning, at the crossing of the

fair, All the glories of that crossing I will share.
Jordan I'll be there, I will share.

TO THEE, O CHRIST, WE EVER PRAY.

Rev. Samuel W. Duffield. Mendelssohn.

1. To thee, O Christ, we ev - er pray, And blend our prayer with tears :
2. Our hearts shall be at rest in thee, In sleep they dream thy praise ;
3. Give us a life that can- not fail! Refresh our spir - its then ;
4. Our vows in song we pay thee still, And, at this evening hour,

Thou pure and ho - ly One, al - way Pro - tect our night of years !
And to thy glo - ry faith- ful - ly They hail the com - ing days.
Let blackest night be - fore thee pale ; And bring thy light to men.
May all that we have purposed ill Be right thro' per - fect power.

IN THAT LAND.

A. H. A.   A. H. A.

1. In that land of light and beau - ty, Where the saints with Je - sus dwell;
2. By the crys- tal sea, where the breez - es Softly blow o'er hear'n's broad plain,
3. There are mansions there, golden mansions, With the light' of God they shine;
4. O the glorious song of the ransomed, How it fills hear'n's mighty dome;

In a glad new song of triumphant praise They his love and glo - ry tell.
Stand the ransomed throng in their robes of white, Sounding forth their sweet refrain.
And the walls resound with the joyous sound Of the saints' glad song di- vine.
O the joy of those who with Je- sus dwell, They are safe with him at home.

CHORUS.

There shall I, by and by, Join the ev - er hap - py
There shall I, by and by,

throng; Giv - ing praise, end - less praise, In a
by and by; Giv - ing praise, end - less praise,

glad, triumphant song, by and by, In a glad, triumphant song, by and by.

WHEN JESUS CALLED ME.

Rev. Johnson Oatman, Jr.   Wm. Edie Marks.

1. I nev-er can for-get the time, When Je-sus called me;
2. My heart was sunk in depths of sin, When Je-sus called me;
3. My feet had wandered far a - stray, When Je-sus called me;
4. I then resolved no more to roam, When Je-sus called me;

His voice more sweet than sil - ver chime, When Je-sus called me.
But O how soon the light broke in, When Je-sus called me.
But soon I found the nar - row way, When Je-sus called me.
I start-ed for my heav'nly home, When Je-sus called me.

Chorus.

When Je-sus called me, When Je-sus called me; I heard him call-ing wan-d'rer come, I'll take thy hand, I'll lead thee home.

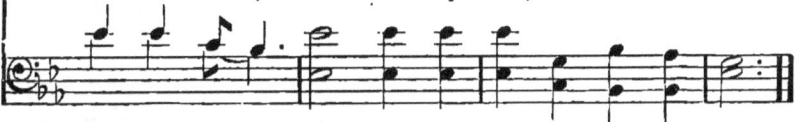

HEAVEN IS MY HOME.

Rev. Thos. R. Taylor.   A. H. A.

1. I'm but a stranger here, Heav'n is my home; Earth is a
2. What tho' the tempest rage? Heav'n is my home; Short is my
3. Therefore I mur-mur not, Heav'n is my home; What-e'er my

des-ert drear, Heav'n is my home; Dan-ger and sorrow stand 'Round me on
pilgrimage, Heav'n is my home; And time's wild, wintry blast Soon will be
earthly lot, Heav'n is my home; And I shall surely stand There at my

ev - 'ry hand; Heav'n is my fath - er - land; Heav'n is my home.
o - ver past; I shall reach home at last; Heav'n is my home.
Lord's right hand; Heav'n is my fath - er - land; Heav'n is my home.

CHORUS.

Home,   beau - ti - ful   home,   Heav'n is my
beautiful home,   beautiful home,

fath - er- land, my home, sweet home; Home, beau - ti - ful
beautiful home,

home, Heav'n is my fath- er- land, my home, sweet home.
beautiful home,

GOD IS LOVE.

Sir John Bowring, LL. D.   E. S. Carter.

1. God is love, his mer- cy brightens All the path in which we rove,
2. Chance and change are bus - y ev - er, Man decays, and a - ges move;
3. Ev'n the hour that dark- est seemeth, Will his changeless goodness prove;
4. He with earth- ly cares en- twineth Hope and com- fort from a - bove;

Bliss he wakes and woe he lightens; God is wisdom, God is love.
But his mer- cy wan - eth nev- er; God is wisdom, God is love.
From the gloom his brightness streameth; God is wisdom, God is love.
Ev -'rywhere his glo - ry shineth; God is wisdom, God is love.

I WANT TO GO HOME WHEN I DIE.

Rev. Johnson Oatman, Jr.

Geo. C. Hugg.

1. I want to go home when I die, To mansions be-
2. I want to go home when I die, Where God wipes all
3. I want to go home when I die, For mansions in
4. I want to go home when I die, I long for the
5. I want to go home when I die, To live while the

yond the blue sky; There to walk in the light Of that
tears from the eye; There to lean on his breast, And for
glo - ry I sigh; For my treas - ure is there, In those
hour to draw nigh When life's sor - rows shall cease And my
a - ges shall fly; With life's bur - dens all past, I shall

coun - try so bright, I want to go home when I die.
ev - er- more rest, I want to go home when I die.
por - tals so fair, I want to go home when I die.
soul find re - lease, I want to go home when I die.
find rest at last, I want to go home when I die.

Chorus.

I want to go home, I want to go home, To

rest in that home of the soul; Where saints walk in white, Where no

sor-row can blight, While the years of e - ter - ni - ty roll.

FATHER, HOLY FATHER.

AUTHOR NOT KNOWN.

G. HINTON.

1. Fa - ther, ho - ly Fa - ther, Now the sun has come,
2. We thy lit - tle chil - dren, To thy throne a - bove
3. Thou art wise and lov - ing, Thou art great and strong;
4. Hear us, ho - ly Fa - ther, As to thee we pray,
5. Fa - ther, God, our Fa - ther, Guide us ev - 'ry hour;

Last verse.

Bring-ing light and glo - ry From thy heav'nly home.
We would hymn thy prais - es, We would sing thy love.
Glad when we do right - ly, Grieved when we do wrong.
Ask - ing thee to keep us Safe from harm to - day.
Keep us safe, and shield us. From temp - ta - tion's pow'r. A - men.

62 THE MASTER HAS COME, AND CALLETH FOR THEE.

Rev. Johnson Oatman, Jr.   (John 11: 28.)   W. F. Fowler.

SOLO.

1. When Martha met Christ, when her brother was dead, She straight with the
2. Dear sin- ner, we point you to Cal - va- ry's brow, Where suf -fer- ing
3. Dear Christian, the har- vest fields are now all white, Point souls to that
4. That home up in heav- en is wait- ing for all, A robe and a

Moderato. p

news to her sis - ter did flee; And run- ning up to her, she
there, that dear Christ you may see; He died to re- deem you, O
dear one who died on the tree; Work while it is day, for it
crown waits for you and for me; Great joy for his peo - ple who

ea - ger - ly said, "The Mas - ter has come, and call - eth for thee."
come to him now, "The Mas - ter has come, and call - eth for thee."
soon will be night, "The Mas - ter has come, and call - eth for thee."
an - swer his call, "The Mas - ter has come, and call - eth for thee."

CHORUS.

The Master has come, the Master has come, Come now, go quickly and see ; The

Master has come, the Master has come, He calleth, he calleth for thee.

* Omit last time.

LORD, THY WORD ABIDETH.

REV. H. W. BAKER.   W. BOYD.

1. Lord, thy word a - bid - eth,   And our footsteps guid - eth ;
2. When the storms are o'er us,   And dark clouds be - fore us,
3. Word of mer - cy, giv - ing   Suc - cor to the liv - ing ;
4. Oh, that we dis - cern - ing   Its most ho - ly learn - ing,

Who its truth be - liev - eth   Light and joy re - ceiv - eth.
Then its light di - rect - eth,   And our way pro - tect - eth.
Word of life sup - ply - ing   Com - fort to the dy - ing !
Lord, may love and fear thee,   Ev - er - more be near thee !

Rev. Johnson Oatman, Jr.   W. F. Fowler.

March time.

1. O be-hold this val-iant arm-y marching by,...................
2. Look up-on this arm-y as they march a-long,...................
3. Where this arm-y march-es, clouds all dis-ap-pear,...........
4. Come and join this arm-y, be a sol-dier true,................

O be-hold this val-iant arm-y march-ing by,

See their ban-ners proud-ly wave to-ward the sky;...............
"All the world for Je-sus" is their bat-tle song;..............
For they car-ry sunshine, hap-pi-ness and cheer;...............
Old or young, a glorious work is wait-ing you;.................

See their ban-ners proud-ly wave to-ward the sky;

Sing-ing as they're marching all a-long the way,...............
Je-sus is their Cap-tain, he will lead them right,.............
Heav-y hearts grow light-er, hope is made to live,.............
Look-ing up and lift-ing up you'll win the prize,.............

Sing-ing as they're march-ing all a-long the way,

Look-ing up and lift-ing up from day to day.
Look-ing up and lift-ing up, they'll win the fight.
Bless-ings fall up-on them for the aid they give.
Then a-waits a crown of life a-bove the skies.

CHORUS.

O see the Epworth arm - y marching by, Look up and lift up is their battle cry;

Look up to Je - sus with a faith not dim, Lift up the weak ones, point them to him.

PRAISE TO THEE, THOU GREAT CREATOR!

REV. JOHN FAWCETT, D. D.

J. G. C. STORL.

1. Praise to thee, thou great Cre - a - tor! Praise to thee from ev - 'ry tongue;
2. Fa - ther! source of all com - passion! Pure, un - bounded grace is thine:
3. Praise to God, the great Cre - a - tor, Fa - ther, Son, and Ho - ly Ghost;
4. Joy - ful - ly on earth a - dore him, Till in heav'n our song we raise;

Join, my soul, with ev - 'ry creature, Join the u - ni - ver - sal song.
Hail the God of our sal - va - tion, Praise him for his love di - vine!
Praise him ev - 'ry liv - ing creature, Earth and heav'n's u - ni - ted host.
Then en - raptured fall be - fore him, Lost in won - der, love and praise!

PULL AWAY.

Rev. Johnson Oatman, Jr.   Geo C. Hugg.

1. Sail - ors bound   for   yon - der shore, Pull a - way,   pull a-
2. Send the boat   o'er   yon - der crest, Pull a - way,   pull a-
3. If   to Christ you would prove true, Pull a - way,.   pull a-
4. 'Till your work   on   earth is done, Pull a - way,   pull a-

Pull   a - way,

way ;   Soon   the   voy - age   will   be   o'er, Pull   a-
way ;   This   is   not   the   time   to   rest, Pull   a-
way ;   There's   a   work   for   you   to   do, Pull   a-
way ;   'Till   the   crown   of   life   is   won, Pull   a-

pull   a - way ;

way,   pull a - way.   Though   in   face   of
way,   pull a - way.   If   you   brave - ly
way,   pull a - way.   Whis - per   in   a
way,   pull a - way.   'Till   your   boat   has

Pull   a - way,   pull a - way.

wind and tide, You will all the storms out - ride, Soon will gain the
face the blast, 'Till the storm of life is past, You will rest at
sin - ners ear Words of com - fort, and of cheer ; God will help you,
crossed the foam, Anchored there, no more to roam, 'Till with Je - sus,

oth - er side, Pull a - way, pull a - way.
home at last, Pull a - way, pull a - way.
do not fear, Pull a - way, pull a - way.
safe at home, Pull a - way, pull a - way.

Pull a- way, pull a- way.

CHORUS.

Pull, pull a - way, pull, pull a-
Pull, pull a- way, sail - ors, pull, pull a- way, Pull, pull a- way, sail - ors,

way, 'Till the clos-ing of the day; Keep on working
pull a - way,

as you pray, Pull a - way, pull a - way.

Pull a- way, pull a- way.

IN HIS ARMS, BY AND BY.

Rev. Johnson Oatman, Jr.   Geo. C. Hugg.

1. Lift your eyes, ye pilgrims, toward the promised land, Lift your
2. We will fear no dan - ger as we march a - long, We will
3. Tho' we walk in sor - row and the tear drops fall, Tho' we
4. When our work is fin - ished and our race is run, When our
5. There will be no riv - er when we come to die, There will

eyes, ye pilgrims, toward the promised land; For Je - sus will
fear no dan - ger as we march a - long; For Je - sus will
walk in sor - row and the tear drops fall; Yet Je - sus will
work is fin - ished and our race is run; Then Je - sus will
be no riv - er when we come to die; For Je - sus will

take us in his arms, by and by, And car - ry us safe - ly home.
guide us with his eye all the way, And car - ry us safe - ly home.
send the Comfort - er, bless his name, And car - ry us safe - ly home.
give his toil - ers rest, bless - ed rest, And car - ry us safe - ly home.
take us in his arms, by and by, And car - ry us safe - ly home.

Chorus.

He will car - ry us safe - ly home,   He will
                                        by and by,

car - ry us safe - ly home;
by and by;
Yes, Je - sus will

take us in his arms,............ And car-ry us safe - ly home.
by and by,

THREE IN ONE, AND ONE IN THREE.

Rev. Gilbert Rorison, LL. D.   F. R. Grey.

1. Three in One, and One in Three, Rul - er of the earth and sea,
2. Light of lights; with morning shine; Lift on us thy light di - vine;
3. Light of lights; when falls the even, Let it close on sin forgiven;
4. Three in One, and One in Three, Darkling here we worship thee;

Hear us, while we lift to thee Ho'- ly chant and psalm.
And let char - i - ty be nigh Breathe on us her balm.
Fold us in the peace of heaven, Shed a ves - per calm.
With the saints here - af - ter we Hope to bear the palm.

PRESSING HOMEWARD.

Rev. Johnson Oatman, Jr.   Geo. C. Hugg.

1. I am pressing toward a cit - y that is far beyond the skies, To that
2. I am pressing toward a cit - y where my loved ones watch and wait, They have
3. I am pressing toward a cit - y where the saints for-ev - er stand, As with
4. I am pressing toward a cit - y; brother, won't you go a- long? There is

country which we call the "Promised Land;" When the golden gates are lift- ed, as with
lived in yonder cit - y man- y years; But we'll have a joy- ful meeting when I
joy they sing their great Redeemer's praise; I ex- pect to swell the chorus when I
room for all who wish to en - ter there; There's a robe and crown all read- y; come and

my dear Lord I rise, I will en - ter in to sit at his right hand.
pass the great pearl gate, In that land where God shall wipe a- way all tears.
join that blood-washed band, Then my voice and harp shall ring thro' endless days.
join the ransomed throng, Come and oc - cu - py your mansion bright and fair.

Chorus.

Yes, I'm pressing toward a cit - y nev - er seen by mor - tal men,

That was promised to the seed of A - bra- ham; I am pressing toward a

cit - y called the New Je- ru - sa-lem, I've been washed in the blood of the Lamb.

HOLY BIBLE, BOOK DIVINE.

JOHN BURTON.   R. R. CHOPE.

1. Ho - ly Bi - ble, book di - vine; Precious treasure, thou art mine;
2. Mine, to chide me when I rove; Mine, to show a Saviour's love;
3. Mine, to com-fort in dis- tress, If the Ho -ly Spir - it bless;
4. Mine, to tell of joys to come, And the reb - el sin-ner's doom;

Mine, to tell me whence I came; Mine, to teach me what I am.
Mine art thou to guide my feet, Mine, to judge, condemn, ac - quit.
Mine, to show by liv - ing faith Man can triumph o - ver death.
Ho - ly Bi - ble, book di - vine, Precious treasure, thou art mine.

ETERNITY'S SHORE.

To Rev. H. D. Lowing.

Adam Geibel.   Adam Geibel.

Solo and Quartette.

1. There's a mansion just o - ver the riv - er,   Which my Sav-iour's preparing for
2.   In that mansion just o - ver the riv - er,   Where the saints of all a - ges re -
3. When the jour-ney of life   is com-ple-ted,   When its toil and its warfare is

me;.......... And I know I shall rest there for - ev - er,   When I've
- pose;......... There the Lamb is   resplend-ent for - ev - er,   For the
done;......... When the light of   its day   is re-cede-ing,   And I

cross'd o'er the dark, nar-row sea;.......... And I know I shall meet ma-ny
light of His pur - i - ty glows;........ O I'm longing, and watching, and
bask in its last set-ting sun;.......... Then dear Je - sus, I pray Thee pre -

lov'd ones,   Who have cross'd the dark wa- ters be - fore;   And the
wait - ing,   And my heart yearns to go, more and more;   Ah! what
- pare me,   That to man-sions of bliss I may soar;   And to

Sav-iour I'll see in His glo - ry,   When I land on E-ter-ni-ty's shore.
joy and what rap-ture will greet me,   When I land on E-ter-ni-ty's shore.
Thee will I give all the glo - ry,   When I land on E-ter-ni-ty's shore.

REFRAIN.

mf   *cres.*

When I land on E-ter-ni-ty's shore, When I land on E-ter-ni-ty's shore;

f   *dim.*   *rit.*   *p*

Yes, the Saviour I'll see in His glo - ry, When I land on e-ter-ni-ty's shore.

74   I'LL TRUST IN THEE EVER.

W. S.

Rev. Wm. Stone.

1. All sorrows and joys come un-bidden to me, Life's pleasures and treasures I
2. Why mention the sorrows that burden thy life? Why en - ter the conflict of
3. I'll trust then in Je-sus, for whate'er betides, My sins are all pardoned with

seek not to see; Vain hal - lu - ci - na - tions they ev - er must be, Blest
tem - po - ral strife? Since Je - sus hath said, "It is not bread a-lone." His
blood from his side; Oh, broth- er, if then for our sins he hath died, Thy

Chorus.

Je - sus, my Saviour, to thee would I flee. }
promise is ev - er, I'll pi - lot thee home. } I'll trust in thee ev- er, and
wants, tho' they're many, in Je - sus confide. }

naught shall e'er sev- er, I'm free from the bonds of this world; I read, "God is

love," and now from a- bove Sweetly he whispers and calls me his child.

THE FIRE IS BURNING.

Rev. Johnson Oatman, Jr.   Geo. C. Hugo.

Joyously.

1. I've been on Mount Pisgah's loft- y height, And I've sat - is- fied my longing
2. I will walk with Jesus, bless his name, And to be like him I ev -'ry
3. I my all up-on the al-tar lay, As I to my clos-et loving-
4. By faith's eye I scan the ocean's foam, And beyond I see the ha- ven

heart's de - sire ; For I caught a glimpse of glo-ry bright, And my soul is
day as - pire ; For his love is like a heav'nly flame, And my soul is
ly re - tire ; And the flame consumes while there I pray, And my soul is
I de - sire ;. There I view the beacon lights of home, And my soul is

CHORUS.

burning with the fire. Oh, the fire is burning, yes,'tis brightly burning,

Oh, 'tis burning, burning in my soul; Oh, the fire is burning,

yes, 'tis brightly burning, Oh, 'tis burning, burning in   my   soul.
                                                            burning in my soul.

IT'S FILLING ME.

Rev. Johnson Oatman, Jr.   Adam Geibel.

1. All a - round this ver - y hour, Falls there streams of heav'nly pow'r;
2. Send us show'rs of heav'nly grace, Let Thy pres - ence fill this place;
3. Thou a - lone this pow'r can'st give, With-out which I dare not live;

Fall - ing now so full and free, Praise the Lord, it's fill-ing me.
Speak the word and it shall be, That thy show - ers fall on me.
Give me pow'r to work for thee, Let the stream reach e - ven me.

CHORUS.

Hal - le - lu - jah! feel the pow'r, Fall-ing like a mighty show'r;

Com - ing now so full and free, Praise the Lord, it's fill-ing me.

THE HARBOR-HOME.

77

HARRIET E. JONES.   J. HOWARD ENTWISLE.

1. You're sailing t'ward the fearful rapids, brother, Face the harbor - home! You're
2. Beware of hidden rock and sand, my brother, Face the harbor - home! Oh,
3. Be- fore you there is aw- ful danger, brother, Face the harbor - home! Just

drifting farther from the beacon, brother, Face the harbor-home! See the clouds of
turn toward the shining beacon, brother, Face the harbor-home! Shining stars their
turn about and there is safety, brother, Face the harbor-home! Brightly now the

darkness o'er you, See the man- y wrecks be- fore you, Turn this moment, we im-
watch are keeping, An- gry waves are 'round you sweeping, Guardian an- gels must be
light is burning, Wise are they the light discerning, Oh! at once your back be

CHORUS.

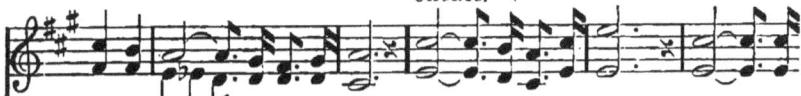

plore you, Face.... the harbor-home! Face... the harbor-home! Face.... the
weeping, Face.... the harbor-home!
turning, Face.... the harbor-home!

Face, O face   Face, O face   the   harbor-home! Face, O face

harbor-home! The light discern, your frail bark turn, And face...... the harbor-home!
the   harbor-home!   quickly face   the   harbor-home!

Copyright, 1896, by John. J. Hood.   face the har - bor - home!

78 THE LORD CAME DOWN TO THE GARDEN OF EDEN.

Rev. Johnson Oatman, Jr. Adam Geibel.

1. The Lord came down to the Gar-den of E-den And walked with A-dam be-
2. Three hundred years he was walking with E-noch, And then God took him with
3. The Lord came down to the three Hebrew children, And in the furnace he
4. Our Lord once walked with dis-ci-ples to Emmaus, And made their sorrows and

neath the tree; In sea-sons of sor-row, when I most need him, Why
him to be; If my heart is long-ing to be more like him, Why
set them free; If he walked with Dan-iel among the li-ons, Why
sadness flee; If he is for-ev-er the same blessed Saviour, Why

Chorus.

will he not come and walk with me? Yes, he will come, O

yes, he will come, When I am needing his sym-pa-thy; When Je-sus

sees me walk-ing in sor-row, Then he will come and walk with me.

THE BLOOD UPON THE DOOR.

Rev. Johnson Oatman, Jr.

Geo. C. Hugg.

Slow, and with great expression.

1. When the Lord pass'd over E-gypt, There was weeping ev-'ry-where, For the
2. We are in a land of danger, And death lurks on ev-'ry hand, But that
3. Not the blood of lambs or cat-tle, Sprinkled o - ver an - y part, But the

an-gel smote the first-born, Of each family dwelling there, But some hous-es
soul has per-fect safe-ty, Who obeys the Lord's command, For se-cure in
blood of Christ the Saviour, Can redeem a hu-man heart, Then when death these

he pass'd o - ver, As his word had said be-fore, And death entered not the
God's pa - vil - ion, He can watch life's breakers roar, For God's angels guard that
ties shall sev- er, And we walk on earth no more, We may live with Christ for -

CHORUS.

por-tals, Where the blood was on the door. }
dwelling, Where the blood is on the door. } Pre-cious blood up - on the door, Sav-ing
ev - er, If *His* blood is on the door. }

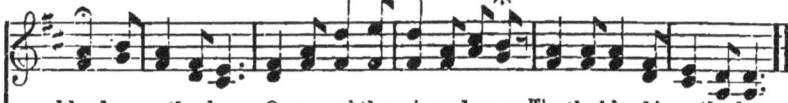

blood up-on the door, O my soul there is no danger, When the blood is on the door.

NO, NOT ONE!

REV. JOHNSON OATMAN, JR.
GEO. C. HUGG.

Slow, and with great feeling.

1. There's not a friend like the low - ly Je-sus, No, not one! no, not one!
2. No friend like Him is so high and ho-ly, No, not one! no, not one!
3. There's not an hour that He is not near us, No, not one! no, not one!
4. Did ev - er Saint find this friend forsake him? No, not one! no, not one!
5. Was e'er a gift like the Sav-iour giv-en? No, not one! no, not one!

None else could heal all our soul's dis- eas- es, No, not one! no, not one!
And yet no friend is so meek and low-ly, No, not one! no, not one!
No night so dark but His love can cheer us, No, not one! no, not one!
Or sin - ner find that He would not take him? No, not one! no, not one!
Will He re-fuse us a home in heav-en? No, not one! no, not one!

CHORUS.

Je - sus knows all a-bout our struggles, He will guide till the day is done,

There's not a friend like the low - ly Je-sus, No, not one! no, not one!

WILL THERE BE ANY STARS?

E. E. HEWITT.　　　　　　　　　　　　　　　JNO. R. SWENEY.

1. I am thinking to-day of that beau-ti-ful land I shall reach when the
2. In the strength of the Lord let me la-bor and pray, Let me watch as a
3. Oh, what joy will it be when his face I behold, Living gems at his

sun go-eth down; When thro' wonderful grace by my Saviour I stand, Will there
win-ner of souls; That bright stars may be mine in the glo-ri-ous day, When his
feet to lay down; It would sweeten my bliss in the cit-y of gold, Should there

CHORUS.

be an-y stars in my crown?
praise like the sea-billow rolls. } Will there be an-y stars, an-y stars in my crown,
be an-y stars in my crown.

When at evening the sun go-eth down?...... When I wake with the blest
goeth down?

In the mansions of rest, Will there be an-y stars in my crown?......
an-y stars in my crown?

Copyright, 1897, by Jno. R. Sweney.

NOW I'M COMING HOME.

Rev. Johnson Oatman, Jr.

Geo. C. Hugg.

With feeling.

1. Long I have wandered a - far from my Lord, Now I am coming home;
2. Tired of the world with its fol - ly and sin, Now I am coming home;
3. Knowing my Saviour can give me his rest, Now I am coming home;
4. Humbly I crave but a poor servant's place, Now I am coming home;
5. Oh, bless the Lord, my dear Saviour I see, Now I am coming home;

Longing to be to his fa - vor restored, Now I am coming home.
Blieving the Saviour will welcome me in, Now I am coming home.
Longing to an - chor my soul on his breast, Now I am coming home.
On - ly de - sir - ing to taste of his grace, Now I am coming home.
Waiting to welcome a sin - ner like me, Now I am coming home.

CHORUS.

Yes, I am coming, Dear Lord, I'm coming, Just now I'm coming home;

Yes, I am coming, Dear Lord, I'm coming, Just now I'm coming home.

O DON'T STAY AWAY.

REV. JOHNSON OATMAN, JR. REV. W. J. STUART, A. M.

With expression.

1. Come soul and find thy rest, No long - er be dis- tress'd;
2. Dark is the world and cold, Her cares can - not be told;
3. Come with thy load of sin, Christ died thy soul to win;
4. Time here will soon be past, Mo - ments are fly - ing fast;
5. Come, O we pray thee, come, Come and no long - er roam;

Come to thy Sav - iour's breast, O don't stay a - way.
Come to thy Sav - iour's fold, O don't stay a - way.
Now He will take thee in, O don't stay a - way.
Judg - ment will come at last, O don't stay a - way.
Come now and start for home, O don't stay a - way.

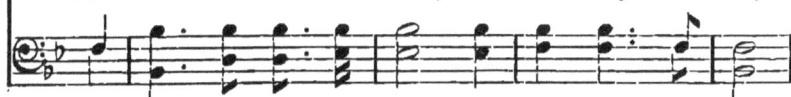

CHORUS.

Pray'rs are as - cend - ing now, An - gels are bend - ing now;

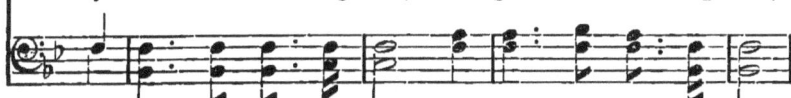

Ritard.....................

Both worlds are blend - ing now, O don't stay a - way.

ONE THING I KNOW.

E. E. HEWITT.   WM. J. KIRKPATRICK.

SOLO OR QUARTET.

1. One thing I know ;...... oh, bless his name,...... To me the Lord........ of mercy
2. One thing I know ;......he heard my cries,...... With mighty pow'r......he touched my
3. One thing I know ;...... he died for me,.........In him my hope,...... my trust shall
4. One thing I know ;...... the Saviour's mine,......'. Oh, boundless grace,...... oh, joy di-
5. One thing I know ;...... oh, help me sing...... Such happy praise...... to Christ our

One thing I know ;   oh, bless his name,   To me, the Lord

came,......... He filled my heart,........ with love's bright flame,........ This I
eyes, ... To see the light .... that nev- er dies,........... This I
be,............ My Saviour lives......... e-ter-nal-ly,............ This I
vine !......... And heav'nly beams........ around me shine,........ This I
King,......... While smiling faith......... and love up-spring,........ This I

of mer-cy came,   He filled my heart   with love's bright flame,

CHORUS.

know,........ this I know. I know, I know,......... he loved me
This I know,   I know, I know,

so,............ He saved my soul........ from sin and woe,........ Now peace and
He loved me so,   He saved my soul   from sin and woe,

joy............ he doth be - stow,......... This I know,........ This I know.
Now peace and joy   he doth bestow,   This I know,

MARCHING ONWARD, CHRISTIAN BAND.

R. B. F.   ROBT. BROOKS FINCH.

With force.

1. Marching on- ward, Christian band, See the hosts from ev -'ry land ;
2. Hosts on hosts, he has de- creed, Shall from Sa - tan yet be freed ;
3. Onward, then, brave Christian band, Tho' temp- ta - tion ye must stand ;

See the tempted and the tried, Martyred throngs on ev - 'ry side ;
Ye have then great work to do. Up ! brave Christians, ev - er true ;
Thro' the night of darkness, soon Ye shall see the morning's bloom—

Strong in faith, they know not fear, Tho' the hoards of sin ap- pear.
Christ the watchword still shall be, With it gain the vic - to - ry.
Christ the Sun shall re - ap- pear, Tho' the night be e'er so drear.

I EXPECT TO GET TO HEAVEN BY THE SAME OLD WAY.

REV. JOHNSON OATMAN, JR.　　　　　　　　　　GEO. C. HUGG.

1. The way our fa - ther's trav-eled　is good e - nough for me,
2. The world may sneer and tell me　I'll nev - er reach the goal,
3. When bowers of sin. en - tice me　to rest my wea - ry feet,
4. Mill-ions are now in glo - ry,　in shin - ing white ar-rayed,

They fol-lowed in　the foot-steps　that led from Cal - va - ry,
That good works are　suf - fi - cient　to save a hu - man soul,
I find in Christ　my Sav-iour,　a safe, a sure re - treat,
Who trav-eled this　same path-way,　and oft - en were dis-mayed,

It led them up　to glo - ry,　that land of end.- less day,
But while the world　is talk - ing,　I still will watch and pray,
He tells me　to press on - ward,　and not look back, nor stay,
But hap - py now　in glo - ry　they sing both night and day,

I ex - pect to get to heav - en by the same old way.
I ex - pect to get to heav - en by the same old way.
I ex - pect to get to heav - en by the same old way.
I ex - pect to get to heav - en by the same old way.

I EXPECT TO GET TO HEAVEN, etc. Concluded.

CHORUS.

O this bless-ed old way, it is good e-nough for me,

Ritard.....................................

It is good e-nough for me, it is good e-nough for me;

a tempo.

My Sav-iour goes be-fore me, I fol-low Him each day,

I ex-pect to get to heav-en by the same old way.

OVER THE SEA.

"And he saith unto them, Follow me, and I will make you fishers of men."
A. F. M. Matthew 5: 19. A. F. MYERS.

Not too fast.

1. Hear the Saviour saying, "Come to me," O - ver the sea of Gal - i - lee;
2. 'Tis the call of mer- cy; heed the voice, O - ver the sea of Gal - i - lee;
3. Turn from sin to Je- sus, trust his word, O - ver the sea of Gal - i - lee;

Sad, erring soul, he gently speaks to thee, O - ver the sea of Gal - i - lee.
Pen - i - tent one, Christ bids thy heart rejoice, O - ver the sea of Gal - i - lee.
Yield to the tones so oft - en sweetly heard, O - ver the sea of Gal - i - lee.

CHORUS.

O- ver the sea, beau- ti - ful sea, Calling to thee,
Over the sea, beautiful sea, Calling to thee,

"Come un- to me," O - ver the sea, beau- ti - ful sea; calling to
"Come unto me,"

thee, "Come un - to me," O - ver the sea, beau- ti - ful sea, of Gal - i - lee.

A GREEN HILL.

Cecil F. Alexander.
With feeling.

Geo. C. Hugg.

1. There is a green hill far a-way, With-out a cit - y wall,
2. He died that we might be for-giv'n, He died to make us good,
3. Oh, dear - ly, dear - ly has he lov'd, And we must love him too,

Where our dear Lord was cru - ci-fied, Who died to save us all;
That we might go at last to heav'n, Sav'd by his pre - cious blood;
And trust in his re-deem-ing blood, And try his works to do;

We may not know, we can - not tell What pains he had to bear,
There was none oth - er good enough To pay the price of sin;
For there's a green hill far a-way, Without a cit - y wall,

But we be-lieve it was for us He hung and suf-fer'd there.
He on - ly could un - lock the gate Of heav'n, and let us in.
Where our dear Lord was cru - ci-fied, Who died to save us all.

MY SONG SHALL BE OF HIM.

REV. JOHNSON OATMAN, JR.   W. F. FOWLER.

1. Tho' oth - er themes some hearts rejoice, Christ fills mine to the brim;
2. While sail - ing o'er the sea of life, He e'er my sail doth trim;
3. I'll praise him in the sunshine bright Or in the shadows dim;
4. And when at last there comes for me The boatman pale and grim;

And while my Sav - iour tunes my voice, My song shall be of him.
In calm or storm, in peace or strife, My song shall be of him.
In morning fair, or dark - est night, My song shall be of him.
Throughout a blest e - ter - ni - ty, My song shall be of him.

CHORUS.

My song,......... my song......... shall be............ of him,.......
My song shall be of him, My song, my song shall be of him,

My song,....... my song......... shall be............ of him;......
My song shall be of him, My song, my song shall be of him;

Let oth - - - ers sing......... some oth- - - - er theme,....
Let oth - ers sing some theme, Let oth-ers sing some oth- er theme,

My song,...... my song...... shall be............ of him.
My song, my song, my song shall be of him.

GRACIOUS SAVIOUR, GENTLE SHEPHERD.

Rev. William H. Havergal.   J. B. Dykes.

1. Gracious Saviour, gen-tle Shep-herd, Lit-tle ones are dear to thee:
2. Ten-der Shepherd nev-er leave us From thy fold to go a-stray;
3. Taught to lisp the ho-ly prais-es Which on earth thy children sing,

Gathered with thine arms, and car-ried In thy bosom may we be.
By thy look of love di-rect-ed, May we walk the narrow way.
May we with thy saints in glo-ry Join to praise our Lord and King.

O COME, GO ALONG.

Rev. Johnson Oatman, Jr.   Adam Geibel.

1. They tell me of a coun - try Where all is bright and fair; Where
2. Our dear ones there are wait - ing To take us by the hand, When
3. The song they sing in heav - en, Be - fore the great white throne, Is

Jesus has a man - sion For all who en - ter there. The streets are filled with
we have passed earth's por - tals And gained that happy land; We'll never know a
just the same old sto - ry That you and I have known. We soon will join the

mu - sic, The courts are filled with song, There's room for you, my brother, there, O
sor - row, For heaven has no wrong, But all is joy for - ev - er, there, O
cho - rus, With voices clear and strong; We'll sing the praise of Jesus there, O

CHORUS.

come, go a - long. O won't you go, my broth - er, To join that

white-robed throng? There's room enough in heav - en, O come, go a - long.

I KNOW THAT JESUS KEEPS.

REV. W. J. STUART, A. M.

GEO. C. HUGG.

1. A - mid the storm that sweeps, Like bil - lows o'er the soul;
2. I will not fear the deeps Of dark-ness nor of pain;
3. There's for the eye that weeps, A rest both sure and sweet;
4. The death that on-ward creeps, Has lost its sting for me;
5. And when I've climb'd the steeps Of heav-en's bright do - main;

I know that Je - sus keeps, That He has full con - trol.
I know that Je - sus keeps, I shall see light a - gain.
I know that Je - sus keeps, I've found a safe re - treat.
I know that Je - sus keeps, His face at last I'll see.
I'll sing that Je - sus keeps, With all the spot-less train.

CHORUS.

He keeps, He keeps, I know He does, He holds me by His pow'r;

He keeps, He saves, I know He does, He's with me ev - 'ry hour.

THE VALLEY OF "NOT TO-DAY."

JESSE P. TOMPKINS.   ADAM GEIBEL.

1. There's a val - ley that leads from the beau - ti - ful hills,
2. There's a mi - rage of lights that al - lure thee a - stray,
3. From a heart of af - fec - tion, so ten - der and true,
4. Flee, O flee as a bird from the val - ley, I pray,

Far a - way from the flow of the heav - en - ly rills,
And so frail are the flow - ers that bloom in the way,
There's a voice in the val - ley that's plead - ing with you,
To the mount - ain of peace, on the wings of "to - day,"

From the mu - sic that floats from the E - den of rest,
Yet you're slight - ing the bea - con that's beam - ing a - bove,
"There is dan - ger," It whis - pers, "if still you de - lay,
There's a ref - uge for you in the rock of His care,

And the man - sions pre - pared in the Home of the blest.
'Tis the beau - ti - ful light of Om - ni - po - tent love.
And the sha - dows of night at the end of the way.
And a path to the cit - y e - ter - nal - ly fair.

'Tis the val-ley of "Not to - day," ...... That is lead-ing thy

soul a - stray, ... O the seed that is sown, And the

tares that have grown, In the val - ley of "Not to - day." ...

I'M GOING HOME TO DIE NO MORE.

Wm. Hunter, D. D.   Arranged.

1. { My heav'nly home is bright and fair; Nor pain, nor death can en-ter there: }
{ Its glitt'ring tow'rs the sun out-shine; That heav'n-ly man-sion shall be mine. }

Cho. { I'm go-ing home, I'm go-ing home, I'm go-ing home to die no more! }
{ To die no more, to die no more, I'm go-ing home to die no more! }

2. My Father's house is built on high,
Far, far above the starry sky:
When from this earthly prison free,
That heavenly mansion mine shall be.

3. While here, a stranger far from home,
Affliction's waves may round me foam;
Although like Lazarus, sick and poor,
My heavenly mansion is secure.

4. Let others seek a home below,
Which flames devour, or waves o'erflow
Be mine a happier lot to own
A heavenly mansion near the throne.

5. Then fail this earth, let stars decline,
And sun and moon refuse to shine,
All nature sink and cease to be,
That heavenly mansion stands for me.

96 — TELL IT OVER AGAIN.

"The time is fulfilled, and the kingdom of God is at hand; repent ye, and believe
A. ROSALTHE CAREY.   the gospel."—Mark 1: 15.   WM. J. KIRKPATRICK.

1. It is new, it is new ev-'ry mo-ment, Half its marvels have
2. 'Tis a message of boun-ty and mer - cy, Full of heart-throbs of
3. It has balm for the wounds of life's bat - tle, For the great Healer
4. Hap-py souls, hap-py souls that re-ceive it, They have on - ly to

nev - er been told; This glad mes - sage of hope and re-demp-tion,
love from the throne; They who quaff at its foun-tain of prom - ise,
left it be - low; And it tells how the heart, sin makes crim-son,
learn and be-lieve; Just to turn from earth-i - dols to Je - sus,

CHORUS.

This sweet gos-pel that nev-er grows old.   Tell it o - ver and
Make the glo-ries of heaven their own.
Grows, by faith in his blood, white as snow.
Keep his word, and sal-va-tion receive.   o-ver and o-ver,

o - ver, Tell it o - ver a - gain;   Tell of
o-ver and o - ver, O-ver and o-ver a-gain, and again;

mer-cy and love and sal - va - tion, Till all earth shall reply, a - men!
mercy and love.

Rev. Johnson Oatman, Jr.

Geo. C. Hugg.

1. "Worthy is the Lamb," the hosts of heaven sing, As be- fore the throne they
2. Worthy is the Lamb who shed his precious blood To restore a world to
3. Worthy is the Lamb, the bleeding sac- ri - fice Who for Adam's race paid
4. "Worthy is the Lamb" let men and angels sing, "Worthy is the Lamb," let

make his praises ring; "Worthy is the Lamb the book to o - pen wide,
hap- pi- ness and God; "When no eye could pit - y and no arm could save,"
such a fear- ful price; Worthy is the Lamb, the paschal Lamb of God,
hal - le - lu- jahs ring; And when life is past, up - on the golden shore,

* Chorus.

Worthy is the Lamb who once was cru- ci - fied."
Je - sus, for our ran - som, himself free- ly gave.
For the world received "Redemption thro' his blood."
"Worthy is the Lamb," we'll shout for- ev - er- more.

Oh, this bleeding Lamb,

oh, this bleeding Lamb, Oh, this dy- ing Lamb, he was found worthy ; Oh, this

bleeding Lamb, Oh, this bleeding Lamb, Oh, this dy- ing Lamb, he was found worthy.

* Chorus arranged from a spiritual.

Rev. Johnson Oatman, Jr.   Adam Geibel.

1. I came to Je-sus sick and poor, He led me to a fountain pure;
2. I prayed to him for a clean heart, From which all e - vil should depart;
3. All that is good my Lord will give, I on - ly ask and I receive;
4. He'll care for me while here I stay, And then I'll live with him al- way;

And since I plunged be - neath its tide, Praise God, my needs are all supplied.
And ev- en while I prayed, I cried, "Praise God, my needs are all supplied.
His love is free, his mercy wide, Praise God, my needs are all supplied.
I'll shout, while crossing Jordan's tide, "Praise God, my needs are all supplied.

CHORUS.

O praise the Lord, I've found a friend Who will go with me to the end;

And while I walk at his dear side, Praise God, my needs are all supplied.

TAKE OFF THE OLD COAT. 99

REV. JOHNSON OATMAN, JR.   GEO. C. HUGG.

1. The feast is prepared, you're urged to come in, Long years you have worn that old coat of sin; But for such a feast this old garment won't do, Then take off the old coat, put on the new.

2. The old coat has brought you sorrow and care, It led you to shame, it led to des-pair; It nev-er has been a bless-ing to you, Then take off the old coat, put on the new.

3. The old coat is soiled with-out and with-in, All covered with guilt, all spot-ted with sin; To wear to the ban-quet it nev-er will do, Then take off the old coat, put on the new.

4. The new coat is love-ly, spot-less, and pure, Ar-rayed in that coat, a welcome is sure; A place at the feast will be sav-ed for you, Then take off the old coat, put on the new.

CHORUS.

O take off the old coat, put on the new, For Christ has a gar-ment ready for you; White robes of Sal-va-tion wait at the door, Then take off the old coat, wear it no more.

LIFE'S RAILWAY TO HEAVEN.

Respectfully dedicated to Railroad Men.

M. E. ABBEY. CHARLIE D. TILLMAN.

SOLO OR DUET. *Tempo ad lib.*

1. Life is like a mountain rail-road, With an en-gi-neer that's brave;
2. You will roll up grades of tri-al; You will cross the bridge of strife;
3. You will oft-en find obstructions; Look for storms of wind and rain;
4. As you roll a-cross the tres-tle, Spanning Jor-dan's swelling tide,

We must make the run suc-cess-ful, From the cra-dle to the grave;
See that Christ is your con-duc-tor, On this light-ning train of life;
On a fill, or curve, or tres-tle, They will al-most ditch your train;
You be-hold the U-nion De-pot, In-to which your train will glide;

Watch the curves, the fills, the tun-nels; Nev-er falt-er, nev-er quail;
Always mind-ful of ob-struction, Do your du-ty, nev-er fail;
Put your trust a-lone in Je-sus; Nev-er fal-ter, nev-er fail;
There you'll meet the Superintendant, God the Fa-ther, God the Son,

Rit.

Keep your hand up-on the throt-tle, And your eye up-on the rail.
Keep your hand up-on the throt-tle, And your eye up-on the rail.
Keep your hand up-on the throt-tle, And your eye up-on the rail.
With the heart-y, joy-ous plau-dit, "Wea-ry pil-grim, welcome home."

LIFE'S RAILWAY TO HEAVEN. Concluded.

CHORUS.

Bless - ed Sav - iour, Thou wilt guide us, Till we reach that bliss-ful shore;

Where the an - gels wait to join us, In Thy praise for - ev - er - more.

I DO BELIEVE.

REV. CHARLES WESLEY.   Unknown.

FINE.

1. Fath - er, I stretch my hands to Thee, No oth - er help I know;
2. What did thine on - ly Son en-dure, Be - fore I drew my breath;
3. O Je-sus, could I this be-lieve, I now should feel thy pow'r;
4. Au - thor of faith, to Thee I lift, My wea - ry, long - ing eyes;

CHO.—I do be-lieve, I now be-lieve, That Je - sus died for me;

D. S.

If Thou withdraw Thy - self from me, Ah, whither shall I go?
What pain, what la - bor to se-cure My soul from end-less death?
And all my wants Thou wouldst relieve, In this ac - cept-ed hour.
Oh, let me now re - ceive that gift; My soul with-out it dies.

And thro' His blood, His precious blood, I shall from sin be free.

SEEK HIM NOW.

JESSE P. TOMPKINS.

GEO. C. HUGG.

With feeling.

1. Are you waiting, on - ly waiting Till the race of life is run?
2. Are you feeding, on - ly feeding On the husk of worldly joys?
3. Are you waiting, on - ly waiting Till your bark shall slow-ly glide

Are you watching, on - ly watching For the set - ting of the sun?
Are you playing, i - dly playing With life's brightly gild - ed toys?
O'er the sol- emn, si - lent riv - er To that land be- yond the tide?

Does the ten- der voice of mer - cy Touch no chord with- in your soul?
Are you lay - ing up no treasure In that land be - yond the veil,
Will you slight the hand of Je - sus When your skies are fair and bright,

.Will you on - ly heed the warning When you're standing at the goal?
Where the joys are ev - er - lasting, And the pleasures nev - er fail?
And then seek him, on - ly seek him At the fad - ing of the light?

SEEK HIM NOW.—Concluded.

Seek   him thou,   seek   him thou,
Seek him thou, O seek him thou, Seek him thou, O seek him thou,

For   the light   is shin - ing now;
For the light is shining now, the light is shining now, just now;

Ere   the cheek   has lost   its bloom
Ere the cheek, the ros - y cheek, in death's dark shade has lost its bloom,

In the shadow of the tomb, Seek him now,   seek   him now.
Seek him now, O seek him now, Seek him now, just now.

I'M GOING HOME.

J. H. E.

J. HOWARD ENTWISLE.

1. I'm go - ing home, I'm go - ing home, A - way from earth's cold cheer,
2. I'm go - ing home, I'm go - ing home, Kind friends will greet me there,
3. I'm go - ing home, I'm go - ing home, A way-ward child I come,

I'm go - ing home, I'm go - ing home, To Heav-en's sun - light clear.
I'm go - ing home, I'm go - ing home, A Sav-iour's love to share.
O, guide me Sav - iour to Thy fold, My blest e - ter - nal home.

CHORUS.

I'm go - ing home, I'm go - ing home, Where many man-sions be,

I'm go - ing home, I'm go - ing home, To spend E - ter - ni - ty.

EMMA A. TIFFANY.   GEO. C. HUGG.

1. Oh, the beau-ti-ful isle of somewhere, That beyond our vis - ion lies ;
2. Oh, the sweet, tranquil isle of somewhere, There the storm-tossed bark finds rest ;
3. Oh, the dear, peaceful isle of somewhere, Near it flows the stream of life ;
4. Oh, the bright, gleaming isle of somewhere, That fair land of lands the best ;

The hand of the ar-tist hath sketched it   In crimson and pur-ple dyes.
With-in the blest harbor its an-chored, No more the wild waves to breast.
Its hills and its vales hath ceased clang-ing With rumblings of war and strife.
'Tis there that the wicked cease troubling, And weary ones are at rest.

Oh, the beau-ti-ful isle of somewhere, Shall we reach it, you and I,
Oh, the sweet, tranquil isle of somewhere, Shall we reach it, you and I,
Oh, the dear, peaceful isle of somewhere, Shall we reach it, you and I,
Oh, the bright, gleaming isle of somewhere, Shall we reach it, you and I,

And bask in the radiant sun-light Of the glorious by and by?.........
                                                        by and by ?

ON THE CROSS.

Selected.

Solo.

Andante.

C. Austin Miles.

Quartet.

Ral - len - tan - do.

1. Be hold! behold! the Lamb of God, On the cross, on the cross;
2. Come, sin- ners, see him lift - ed up, On the cross, on the cross;
3. 'Tis done! the might-y deed is done, On the cross, on the cross;
4. Wher - e'er I go, I'll tell the sto-ry Of the cross, of the cross;

a tempo.

Ral - len - tan - do.

For you he shed his precious blood, On the cross, on the cross.
For you he drinks the bit- ter cup, On the cross, on the cross.
The bat - tle fought, the vic'try won, On the cross, on the cross.
In noth- ing else my soul shall glo- ry, Save the cross, save the cross.

a tempo.

Now hear his ag - o - niz-ing cry, "E - loi Lama Sa - bac - than - i;"
To heav'n he turns his languid eye, "'Tis finished," now the conqu'ror cries,
The rocks do rend, the mountains quake, While Je - sus doth a - tonement make,
Yes, this my constant theme shall be, Thro' time and in e - ter - ni - ty,

Ral - len - tan - do.

pp

Draw near and see your Sav - iour die On the cross, on the cross.
Then bows his sa- cred head and dies On the cross, on the cross.
While Je - sus suf- fers for your sake On the cross, on the cross.
That Je - sus suffered death for me On the cross, on the cross.

HALLELUJAH FOR THE BLOOD! 107

"The blood of Jesus Christ His Son, cleanseth us from all sin."—I. JOHN 1: 7.

A. F. M.   A. F. MYERS.

Spirited.

1. The blood of Je-sus cleans-eth me; Hal-le-lu-jah, hal-le-lu-jah!
2. And with ten thousand, thou-sand tongues; Hal-le-lu-jah, hal-le-lu-jah!
3. The theme demands an an-gel's tongue; Hal-le-lu-jah, hal-le-lu-jah!
4. The grandest theme thro' a-ges rung; Hal-le-lu-jah, hal-le-lu-jah!

That pre-cious blood was shed for thee; Hal-le-lu-jah for the blood!
We'll join this ev-er-last-ing song; Hal-le-lu-jah for the blood!
Which shall be sung in end-less song; Hal-le-lu-jah for the blood!
The grand-est song the world e'er sung; Hal-le-lu-jah for the blood!

CHORUS.

Hal-le-lu-jah, hal-le-lu-jah, Hal-le-lu-jah for the blood;

The blood of Je-sus cleans-eth me; Hal-le-lu-jah for the blood!

A. F. Myers, Toledo, O. Owner of copyright.

THE OLD-TIME POWER.

Rev. Johnson Oatman, Jr.   Geo. C. Hugg.

1. O Lord, re - vive the old-time power, Thy peo- ple need a mighty shower;
2. The power that in the soul was felt; The power that made the heart to melt;
3. The power that did the pris- on shake; The power that made the-sin-ner quake;
4. Lord, for that power we look to thee, The power that made the blind to see;
5. O bless - ed Lord, to thee we pray, O fill us with that power to-day;

The power our fa- thers used to know, Lord, send the power of long a - go.
The power that caused the tear to flow; Lord, send that power of long a - go.
That answered to E - li- jah's call; Lord, let that power up- on us fall.
The power that made the lame to leap, The deaf to hear, the dumb to speak.
Then we for thee will rise and shine, And all the glo - ry shall be thine.

CHORUS.

The old-time power, the old-time power, O send it, Lord, this ver - y hour;

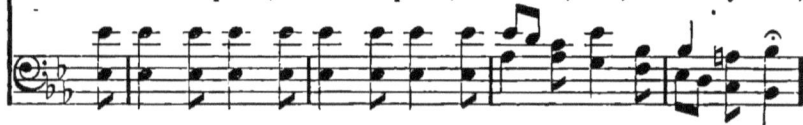

Let not the old-time power be lost, Lord, send the fire of Pen - te- cost.

MY HOME IS ON THE ROCK.

REV. JOHNSON OATMAN, JR.   ADAM GEIBEL.

1. Praise God, I live in Beu-lah land, My House will all the storms withstand;
2. When trials of life come thick and fast, When clouds are o'er my pathway cast;
3. When troubles come that would appall, When other buildings round me fall;
4. And when my time has come to die, I'll have a mansion in the sky;

It is not built on sink-ing sand, My Home is on the rock.
Se-cure, I can withstand the blast, My Home is on the rock.
I rest in Christ my all in all, My Home is on the rock.
But still I'll sing as a-ges fly, My Home is on the rock.

CHORUS.

My Home is on the rock, The ev-er-last-ing rock;

I do not fear when storms are near, My Home is on the rock.

SWELL THE BLOOD-WASHED CHORUS.

REV. JOHNSON OATMAN, JR.   ADAM GEIBEL.

1. Our friends are gath'ring one by one, Up - on the hills of glo - ry;
2. To sing the praise of Je - sus here, The weak-est saint re - joic - es;
3. Our dar-ling child-ren too are there, Their lit - tle voi - ces ring-ing;
4. The saints are there from ev - 'ry land, From ev - 'ry age and na - tion;
5. There's room enough for you and me, And we've an in - vi - ta - tion;

We'll join them when our work is done, And sing redemption's sto - ry.
How must it sound when loud and clear, We join those heav'nly voi - ces.
We'll meet them in that land so fair, And join with them in sing - ing.
They sing as they join hand in hand, The sto - ry of sal - va - tion.
To come and join that com - pa - ny, Of song and ad - o - ra - tion.

CHORUS.

Sing on, sing on un - til we come, And swell the blood-wash'd cho - rus;

How glad the song at "home sweet home" With lov'd one gone before us.

HEAL ME NOW.

Jesse P. Tompkins.   Geo. C. Hugg.

1. Sav-iour give, oh, give me rest   For this torn and troubled breast;
2. Come, oh, come, with me   a-bide, Let me feel thy blood applied;
3. If   I aught withhold from thee, Break the bond and set   me free;
4. Now, just now, I   feel the flood, 'Tis the ev - er precious blood;

Sin has bound me with its chain, Come thou Lamb for sin-ners slain.
Hum-bly at thy feet   I bow, In my weakness heal me now.
Come and bid all sin   de-part, Stamp thine im - age on my heart.
I   am thine, and this is bliss, 'Tis thy re - con - cil - ing kiss.

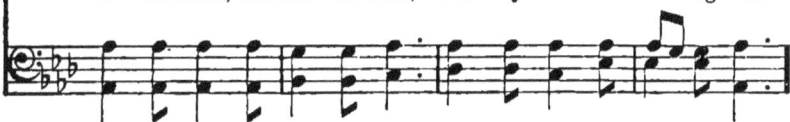

Chorus.

Sav - iour heal, oh, heal me now, As be - fore thy throne I bow;

All my tears can - not re-deem, Plunge me in the crim - son stream.

112 O TASTE AND SEE THE LORD IS GOOD.

W. S. Rev. William Stone.

Firmly.

1. There is a life of bliss di-vine That all may taste and all may find;
2. There is a joy which fills each heart, In it the trials of life de-part;
3. There is a hope that thrills the soul, In him whose heart is perfect, whole;
4. O God, thou giv-er of it all, In Je-sus' name on thee we call;

There is a pow'r that cancels sin, And need-y souls may bathe there-in.
There is a constant peace within, The heart en-tire-ly purged from sin.
There is a hap-pi-ness; O take! Which e'en star-va-tion cannot shake.
Thy sa-cred word in us in-still, Come, Ho-ly Ghost, our hearts to fill.

Chorus.

O taste and see.............. the Lord is good,........... And waits to
O taste and see   the Lord is good,

save........... whoev-er should......... Up-on his name........ for mercy
And waits to save   whoever should   Upon his name

rit.

call;........ O make him now.......... thine all in all............
for mercy call;   O make him now   thine all in all.

THERE IS SUN-LIGHT OVER HEAD.

Rev. Johnson Oatman, Jr.   Adam Geibel.

1. Tho' when walking down life's val-ley, Oft the vale is fill'd with dread;
2. Tis the sun that makes the shadows, So no mat-ter where we tread;
3. In this world of sin and sor-row, Trials on ev-'ry hand are spread;
4. When at last I walk the val-ley, And the shad-ow of the dead;

Yet when e'er I look a-bove me, There is sun-light o-ver head.
Let us sing when days are gloomy, There is sun-light o-ver head.
Yet my heart keeps singing ev-er, There is sun-light o-ver head.
My dear Lord will whisper to me, There is sun-light o-ver head.

CHORUS.

Just a-bove the sun is shin-ing, Then no more the shadows dread;

But re-mem-ber when re-pin-ing, There is sun-light o-ver head.

SATISFIED.

HORATIUS BONAR.

GEO. C. HUGG.

1. When I awake in the sweet morn of morns, After whose dawning night ne'er returns:
2. When I shall meet with the ones I have lov'd, Clasp in my arms the long, long remov'd,
3. When I shall gaze on the dear face of Him, Who died for me, with eye no more dim,

And with whose glory the day ev - er burns, I shall be sat - is - fied.
And find how faithful the Lord then has proved, I shall be sat - is - fied.
And praise Him ever with heaven's swelling hymn, I shall be sat - is - fied.

CHORUS.

I shall be sat - is - fied; I shall be sat - is - fied;
I shall be satisfied, I shall be satisfied,

When in the like-ness of God I'm ar-rayed, I shall be sat - is - fied.

I'LL SING HIS PRAISE.

JESSE P. TOMPKINS.   ADAM GEIBEL.

1. My Saviour, I would sing his praise, The leading light of all my days;
2. My shepherd, I would know his voice, And feed in pas - tures of his choice;
3. My comfort I would hold his hand, When in the vale of grief I stand;
4. My pi- lot, I would have him nigh, When life's last sun - set tints the sky;

He smoothes the roughest path for me, And guides me when I cannot see.
He leads where flow the waters still, When simply I o - bey his will.
He wipes the tear drops from my eyes, And tells of bliss be- yond the skies.
His hand will guide my bark aright O'er death's dark sea to fadeless light.

CHORUS.

I'll sing his praise thro' end- less days, For all his love to me;

I'll sing his praise in sweetest lays, Thro' all e - ter - ni - ty.

PROVE THE CHRIST WITHIN YOU.

Ida L. Reed.   Geo. C. Hugg.

1. From day to day, A - long your way, Prove the Christ with- in you;
2. Thro' darkened ways, Thro' lone- ly days, Prove the Christ with- in you;
3. From paths of sin, Strive souls to win, Prove the Christ with- in you;
4. Thro' grief's dark maze, Send hope's glad rays, Prove the Christ with- in you;

In all you do, To him be true, Prove the Christ with- in you.
Let love's clear light Shine true and bright, Prove the Christ with- in you.
With lov - ing cheer Bring heav- en near, Prove the Christ with- in you.
Let noth -ing dim Your faith in him, Prove the Christ with- in you.

CHORUS.

Prove the Christ with - in you, Prove the Christ with - in you;

In thought, and word, or deed you do, Prove the Christ with- in you.

HORATIUS BONAR.

GEO. C. HUGG..

1. Lord, give me light to do Thy work, For on - ly, Lord, from Thee
2. The way is nar - row, of - ten dark, With lights and shadows strewn :
3. Oh, send me light to do Thy work! More light, more wis-dom give;
4. The work is Thine, not mine, O Lord; It is Thy race we run;

Can come the light, by which these eyes The way of life can see.
I wan - der oft, and think it Thine, When walking in my own.
Then shall I work Thy work in - deed, While on Thine earth I live.
Give light! and then shall all I do, Be well and tru - ly done.

CHORUS.

Send me light! send me light! Light a-long the toilsome way !
Send me light, send me light,

Send me light, dear Lord, that I may labor on, Till I rest in e - ter-nal day.

118

RESIGNATION.

MRS. EMMA A. TIFFANY. ADAM GEIBEL.

1. I stood face to face with a sor-row,...... That threatened my
2. I rode o'er a tempest-rock'd bil-low,...... Which threatened my
3. O'er my soul death's shadows were creep-ing,...... That threatened my

bark to o'er-whelm, But peace float-ed in on the mor-row,......
life to o'er-whelm, But I sweet-ly slept on my pil-low,......
faith to o'er-whelm, But the an-gels, a vig-il were keep-ing,......

REFRAIN.

My Fa-ther was guid-ing the helm. My Fa-ther was guiding the
My Fa-ther was guid-ing the helm. My Fa-ther was guiding the
My Fa-ther was guid-ing the helm. My Fa-ther was guiding the

helm,...

helm, the helm, My Fa-ther was guid-ing the helm, But peace float-ed
helm, the helm, My Fa-ther was guid-ing the helm, But I sweet-ly
helm, the helm, My Fa-ther was guid-ing the helm, But the an-gels a

in on the mor - row,...... My Fa - ther was guid-ing the helm.
slept on my pil - low,...... My Fa - ther was guid-ing the helm.
vig - il were keep-ing,...... My Fa - ther was guid-ing the helm.

SAVIOUR, I COME.

IDA L. REED.

ADAM GEIBEL.

1. Sav - iour, I come to Thee, On Thee I call, Thou art my
2. Sav - iour, I come to Thee, Give me I pray, Thro' Thy great
3. Sav - iour, I come to Thee, Be Thou my Light, Up - ward my

hope and plea, Je - sus my all; Thou Lord my ref - uge art,
love so free, Strength for each day; Thou know-est all my care,
foot - steps lead, Out of the night; In - to the heav'n - ly day,

Com - fort Thou me, Heal Thou my ach - ing heart, Thine would I be.
Je - sus my King, Know - est the griefs I bear, To Thee I cling.
Bright with Thy love, Lead me, O Lord, I pray, Homeward a - bove.

SAVIOUR, LEAD ME THERE.

Jesse P. Tompkins.

Geo. C. Hugg.

1. There is a land so dear to me, It lies beyond the si - lent sea;
2. There is a land where nev- er fades The rainbow or the summer shades;
3. There is a land where forms so bright Shall nev- er vanish from my sight,
4. There is a land where peace shall bide, Joy flows in one per- pet - ual tide;

Where heights of love I seek in vain, My longing soul shall there at - tain.
Where we, beneath a cloudless sky, Shall view the flow'rs that nev - er die.
And leave af- fection's streams to roll In Alpine torrents on my soul.
And love's fair light shall ev- er beam, And sorrows vanish like a dream.

Chorus.

Saviour, lead, O lead me there, To the fa - ces ev - er fair;

To the forms I long to see, Saviour, hold me close to thee.

E. E. HEWITT.

ADAM GEIBEL.

1. In the midst of temp-ta - tion, In the thick of the fight, In our
2. There the Lamb is the glo - ry, Neither sun, moon, nor star, For the
3. When we pass thro' the val - ley, Where the shadows are dim, If we're

sea - sons of sor - row, When we long for the light; When the sweet links are
Light ev - er - last-ing, Sheds its ra-diance a - far; Let us cling to our
rest - ing in Je - sus, Sweetly lean-ing on Him; Then, to Heav-en's ho -

brok-en, And the ties, true and fond, There's a hope we may cherish Of a
Saviour, Let us strengthen love's bond, As we march to His pal-ace, In the
san - nas, We shall glad-ly re-spond, As we en - ter the por-tals Of the

CHORUS.

bright world be-yond. ⎫
bright world be-yond. ⎬ There's a bright world beyond, Yes, a bright world be -
bright world be-yond. ⎭

yond, Sing, O child-ren of Zi - on, There's a bright world be - yond.

HE SAVED ME TOO.

Rev. Johnson Oatman, Jr.　　　　　　　　　Geo. C. Hugg.

1. Once deep con-vic-tion the Lord on me did roll, My heart was heavy, and
2. Once in a meeting, the pow'r of God was there, Many were shouting His
3. Once we were praying for more of pow'r divine, That in His ser-vice we
4. God has a mansion prepared for you and me, Where we will praise Him, through

anxious for my soul, Friends were converted, by faith sav'd thro' and thro',
Name in praise and pray'r, God gave a bless-ing to those in ev - 'ry pew,
might a-rise and shine, God sent His spir-it, our fire He did re-new,
all e-ter-ni-ty, "I will receive you" His prom-is-es are true,

Chorus.

But while the Lord sav'd oth-ers, He sav'd me too. Yes, He sav'd me too!
But while the Lord bless'd others, He bless'd me too. Yes, He bless'd me too!
But while the Lord fill'd oth-ers, He fill'd me too. Yes, He fill'd me too!
But when the Lord takes oth-ers, He'll take me too. Yes, He'll take me too!

He sav'd me too! While the Lord sav'd oth-ers, He sav'd me too!
He bless'd me too! While the Lord bless'd others, He bless'd me too!
He fill'd me too! While the Lord fill'd oth-ers, He fill'd me too!
He'll take me too! When the Lord takes oth-ers, He'll take me too!

TRUSTING JESUS EVERY DAY.

W. E. M.

WM. EDIE MARKS.

1. Trusting in my Saviour ev-'ry day, Trusting him while on my
2. Trusting Je-sus when strong foes I meet, Trusting him when storms a-
3. Trusting him to all my burdens bear, Trusting him to all my

pil-grim way; Trusting him as moments pass a-way, I am
round me beat; Trusting him to give a safe re-treat, I am
sor-row share; Trusting him to take a-way all care, I am

CHORUS.

Trusting Jesus Christ my Sav-iour. I am trust-ing, trusting ev-'ry day,
trusting, trusting,

I am trust-ing, trusting ev-'ry day; Trusting Je-sus ev-'ry day,
trusting, trusting,

As the moments pass away, I am trusting Je-sus Christ my Sav-iour.

THE TESTING TIME.

Emma A. Tiffany.   Geo. C. Hugg.

1. The test-ing time is ver-y near, When at Christ's bar we must appear;
2. Our secret thoughts will then be known, We can-not then for sin   a-tone;
3. We then may call, but all   in vain, Too late! our guilt will still   remain;
4.   O sinner, come, e'er heaven's door   Is closed, to   o-pen nev-er-more;
5. Then when the testing time doth come, You'll find in heav'n sweet rest and home;

Must ap-pear, must   ap-pear, When at Christ's bar we must   appear.
Sin   a-tone, sin   a-tone, We can-not then for sin   a-tone.
Still re-main, still   re-main, Too late! our guilt will still   remain.
Nev-er-more, nev-er-more, Is closed to   o-pen nev-er-more.
Rest and home, rest and home, you'll find in heav'n sweet rest and home.

CHORUS.

Oh, my   soul, art thou read-y   to ap-pear   At the
                                            to appear,

bar, when the judgment day is   here?   With no   counsel at thy side,
                          surely here?

When the book is   opened wide, Oh, my   soul, art thou ready   to appear?

SAVED THROUGH THE BLOOD.

125

"And the blood of Jesus Christ His Son cleanseth us from all sin."—I. JOHN 1: 7.

A. F. M.   A. F. MYERS.

Spirited.

1. I was once lost in sin, and im - pure with-in, But the Sav-iour said
2. I obeyed then His voice, made the Lord my choice, And He saved my own
3. 'Twas by faith in His word that my voice He heard, And by faith in Him

un - to me, I will cleanse thy soul and thou shalt be made whole, Then He
guilt - y soul, Hal- le - lu - jah! God thro' Je - sus' precious blood, Can
I en - dure, As a child of grace I'll run the Christian race, And the

CHORUS.

spake and I was free. } I am saved......... thro' the blood,......
make the wound-ed whole. } I am saved,   thro' the blood,
prize at last se - cure. }

I am saved thro' Je - sus' blood,......... I am saved from sin, and
Jesus' blood,

f

wretchedness with-in, Hal - le - lu -jah! I am saved thro' the blood.........
the blood.

From "The Searchlight." By permission.

HIS BLOOD IS DROPPING DOWN.

REV. JOHNSON OATMAN, JR.   ADAM GEIBEL.

1. Up - on the cross our Sav-iour died, On Calv'ry's brow was cru - ci - fied;
2. For you the thorns once pierced His brow, He drank the cup we know not how;
3. O sin-ner come to Him to - day, For He hath told you that you may;
4. No long-er then be temp-est toss'd, In Je - sus rest, He paid the cost;

See from His hands, His feet, His side, His blood is drop-ping down.
And for sal - va - tion ev - en now, His blood is drop-ping down.
He'll wash your guilt and sin a - way, His blood is drop-ping down.
And that your soul may not be lost, His blood is drop-ping down.

CHORUS.   down,   down,

His blood is dropping, dropping down, His blood is dropping, dropping down,

O sin - ner get be-neath the Cross, His blood is drop-ping down.

Rev. Johnson Oatman, Jr.   W. F. Fowler.

1. The Great Phy- si - cian came to me, And healed my soul's dis- eas - es;
2. His yoke is eas - y, this I find, He ev - 'ry bur - den eas - es;
3. The things of sin, I once did love, No more my spir - it pleas - es;
4. And when at last the hand of death From sin and sor - row frees us,

O bless his name, he set me free, I'll live and die for Je - sus.
He dai - ly gives me peace of mind, I'll live and die for Je - sus.
My sweet- est joys are from a- bove, I'll live and die for Je - sus.
We'll upward soar, with clos- ing breath, To live on high with Je - sus.

CHORUS.

On wings of faith each day I rise, To catch the heav'nly breez - es;

My soul is pressing toward the skies, I'll live and die for Je - sus.

OH, DON'T YOU HEAR HIM KNOCKING?

Rev. Johnson Oatman, Jr.　　　　　　　　J. Howard Entwisle.

1. A hand all bruised and bleeding is knocking at the door, Is knocking
2. How oft-en when in sickness, your bod-y racked with pain, This knocking
3. While standing by the casket of some de-part-ed friend, With sorrow
4. Why will you keep him knocking? why won't you let him in? He'll o-ver-

at the door of your heart; It is the hand of Jesus, who long has
has resounded in your ears; How often in the night time the knock would
your poor heart was sick and sore; What caused that train of thinking of how your
flow your pathway with de-light; That hand so torn and bleeding will wash a-

CHORUS.

knocked before, Tho' oft you have told him to de-part.
come again, So loud it would fill your soul with fears.
life would end? That hand was then knocking at the door.　} Oh, don't you hear him knocking,
way your sin, Oh, welcome the Saviour in to-night.

knocking at the door? He's knocking at the door to come　in;　He wants an invi-

rit. ad lib.

tation to cross your threshold o'er, Then Jesus will save you from all sin.

ANCHORED.

REV. JOHNSON OATMAN, JR.

GEO. C. HUGG.

1. Once up - on the tide I drift - ed, With no guide to
2. Let the storms sweep o'er life's o - cean, They can do me
3. Here my peace flows like a riv - er, Here my soul o'er
4. When this life be - low is end - ed, I shall an - chor

yon - der shore; But I've found a side once rift - ed,
no more harm; An - chored far from their com - mo - tion,
flows with song; Pray'r and prais - es to the giv - er,
on that shore; Where my prais - es will be blend - ed,

CHORUS.

Where I'm safe for - ev - er - more.
I am rest - ing 'neath His arm.
Fill my glad heart all day long.
With ten - thous-and, thousand more.

I am an-chored, safe - ly

an - chored, An-chored nev - er more to roam, An-chored by the

side of Je - sus, An-chored in the soul's bright home.

130   JESUS HAS OPENED THE DOOR.

REV. JOHNSON OATMAN, JR.   ADAM GEIBEL.

1. Wea - ry and la - den with sin,........ Striv-ing thy sins to give
2. Pray-ing for grace day by day,...... Lov -ing Him still more and
3. Af - ter life's struggles are past,...... Waits there a beau - ti - ful

o'er;...... Soul if thou would'st en - ter in,......... Je - sus has
more;..... Rest in His courts on the way,...... Je - sus has
shore;..... If thou wilt live there at last,...... Je - sus has

CHORUS.   door;.........

o-pened the door.......
o-pened the door....... } Je - sus has o - pened the door, the door;
o-pened the door.......

Je - sus has o - pened the door,...... Free from all sin,

en - ter thou in, Je - sus has o - pened the door.......

IDA L. REED.   GEO. C. HUGG.

1. Go with Christ's own loving spir- it, Seek the err- ing in his name;
2. Bear for him the "cups of wa - ter," By thy lov- ing kindness sweet;
3. Tell them lov- ing - ly of Je - sus, Tell how much he is to thee;
4. With the heal- ing balm of mer- cy, Go with Christlike soul to them;

Tell them of his wondrous mer- cy, Help them each a blessing claim.
By thy ten- der pit - y win them, Lead them to the Master's feet.
How thy heart was won to love him, How his blood hath made thee free.
Tell them of his love un- fail- ing, Win them for his di - a - dem.

CHORUS.

Go with Christ's own loving spir - it, Tell them how he waits to bless

Ev - 'ry err - ing soul who seeks him In his truth and righteous - ness.

132 LORD SEND A GREAT WAVE OF SALVATION.

REV. JOHNSON OATMAN, JR.   ADAM GEIBEL.

1. Lord hear us to - day, O turn not a - way, For
2. As we look a - round, how ma - ny are found, Now
3. We thank Thee dear Lord, that Thou in Thy word, Hast
4. We read that at last, when this life is past, There
5. When this life is o'er, may we on that shore, U -

sin has caused great des - o - la - tion, For Thy aid to - day,
liv - ing in sin's deg - ra - da - tion, O help us to win
giv - en a great rev - e - la - tion, We read "God is love,"
will come a great sep - e - ra - tion, One that nev - er ends,
nite in the great ju - bi - la - tion, But while here we stay,

we earn - est - ly pray, Lord send a great wave of sal - va - tion.
them from paths of sin, Lord send a great wave of sal - va - tion.
so now from a - bove, Lord send a great wave of sal - va - tion.
O save our dear friends, Lord send a great wave of sal - va - tion.
we'll pray night and day, Lord send a great wave of sal - va - tion.

CHORUS.

Dear Lord send a wave, poor sin - ners to save, O

may it sweep o'er ev - 'ry na - tion, May it as it rolls,

en - gulf ma - ny souls, Lord send a great wave of sal - va - tion.

DUKE STREET.

John Needham.   John Hatton.

1. A-wake, my tongue, thy tribute bring, To Him who gave thee pow'r to sing;
2. How vast His knowledge! how profound! A deep where al' our thoughts are drowned;
3. Thro' each bright world above, be-hold, Ten thousand thousand charms unfold,
4. But in re-demp-tion, O what grace! Its wonders, O what thought can trace,

Praise Him who is all praise a - bove, The source of wis - dom and of love.
The stars He numbers and their names, He gives to all those heav'nly flames.
Earth, air, and mighty seas com - bine To spead His wis - dom all di - vine.
Here wis-dom shines for - ev - er bright; Praise Him, my soul, with sweet delight,

134 ALL THE WORLD FOR JESUS.

W. E. M.   WM. EDIE MARKS.

1. Onward, Christian army,'tis the Lord's command, Go ye forth and conquer, conquer
2. Nations now are burdened with their load of sin, Sa-tan has dominion, all is
3. Onward, then, till vict'ry shall your efforts crown, Till the haunts of sin are ev-'ry-

ev-'ry land; Tell to all the tidings, spread the news around Of this great sal-
dark with-in; Go and break their fetters, and their bonds destroy, Tell them where to
where cast down; "All the world for Jesus," shout it o'er and o'er, Let it ring a-

CHORUS.

vation where'er man is found.
find e-ternal light and joy. } On, on to vic-to-ry, 'tis the Lord's command,
loud above the battle's roar.

On, on to vic-to-ry, conquer ev-'ry land; Tell them of the Saviour,

of the life he gave That the sons of men e-ter-nal life might have.

SO GOOD.

Rev. Johnson Oatman, Jr.

Geo. C. Hugg.

1. Each time I read the Bi - ble New beauties I can see, I
2. Yes, since I found the Sav - iour I'm hap-py all day long, He
3. And when this life is end - ed, I have a mansion fair Where

love to read of Je- sus Who gave his life for me; I read that my re-
fills my soul with sunshine, He fills my heart with song; I cannot keep from
I shall see my Saviour And live for - ev - er there; And with the saints in

demption Was purchased by his blood, O glo - ry, hal - le- lu - jah, Oh, this
singing, Nor would I, if I could; For when I sing of Je - sus, Oh, it
glo - ry I'll sing a- bout the blood ; Whene'er I think of heaven, Oh, it

CHORUS.

makes me feel so good. It makes me feel so good, Yes, it makes me feel so good ;

This old - en time re - li - gion, Oh, it makes me feel so good.

136

THE VALLEY OF ELIM.

And they came to Elim, where were twelve wells of water, and three-score and ten palm-trees, and they encamped there by the water.—EXODUS 15 : 27.

REV. JOHNSON OATMAN, JR.

GEO. C. HUGG.

With expression.

1. When Israel's hosts were marching across the burning sand, They reach'd a spot
2. They rest-ed there a few days, the cloud moved on ahead, They bade good-bye
3. We have our fami-ly cir-cle, death en-ters at the door, And takes a - way
4. We're on our way to heav-en, that E-lim of the blest, Where we shall dwell

call'd E-lim in that wild des-ert land, Cool wa-ter found for thirs-ty, and
to E-lim, and follow'd where it led, So 'tis with us in this life - like
our lov'd ones, to that blest E-lim shore; We're go-ing on to meet them, no
for-ev - er, and find e - ter-nal rest, I there shall see my Saviour, who

palm-trees waving tall, Sweet pastures for the cat-tle and needed rest for all.
pilgrims here we roam, And pitch our tents at evening, a days march nearer home.
wea-ry march of sand, Will ev - er tire the pilgrims, to hap-py E-lim land.
died to save my soul, I'll nev-er leave that E-lim, while endless a-ges roll.

CHORUS.

In the val - ley of E - lim there is wa - ter, And palm-trees

wav-ing in the sun, We'll sit down be-neath their cooling shad-ow,

And rest when our day's work is done, And rest when our day's work is done.

GOLDEN MOMENTS.

REV. W. J. STUART, A. M.   REV. W. J. STUART, A. M.

1. Gold-en mo-ments now are pass-ing, Soon will end life's lit - tle day,

FINE.

Why not seek for joys e'er-last-ing, Choose you now the bet - ter way;

D.S.—Love is now your heart en - treat-ing, Pointing to a home on high.

D.S.

All be-low is ev - er fleet-ing, Earth can nev - er sat - is - fy,

2. Can you longer slight the blessing
   Of the Saviour of mankind?
Soon will come the time distressing
   When you'll not the Saviour find;
For you can the Spirit grieving,
   Sin away your day of grace,
Why be longer unbelieving?
   Come and take your blood-bought place.

3. Now's the time, the Saviour's waiting
   To bestow His love on you,
Come, no more excuse be making,
   He will bear you conqueror through;

Yield; and sin to Him confessing,
   You will find His Word is true,
He will give you now the blessing
   Of a heart made white and new.

4. And when time with you has ended,
   To a mansion and a throne,
He will take the soul befriended,
   As His loved one and His own;
There you'll bask in life eternal,
   Hard before the throne of gold,
There you'll sing the songs immortal,
   To the ransomed never old.

HE'S ALTOGETHER LOVELY.

REV. JOHNSON OATMAN, JR.   ADAM GEIBEL.

1. A roy - al guest stands at the door, He's al - to- geth - er love - ly;
2. There's naught a-bout him to condemn, He's al - to- geth - er love - ly;
3. His eyes are brighter far than day, He's al - to- geth - er love - ly;
4. Tho' looked at hu- man or divine, He's al - to- geth - er love - ly;
5. I'll sing, while here on earth I stay, He's al - to- geth - er love - ly;

None such was ev - er seen be- fore, He's al - to- geth - er love - ly.
Fair- est among the sons of men, He's al - to- geth - er love - ly.
His smile is sweeter far than May, He's al - to- geth - er love - ly.
Ten thousand beauties 'round him shine, He's al - to- geth - er love - ly.
And then I'll sing thro' end - less day, He's al - to- geth - er love - ly.

CHORUS.

Al - to- geth - er love - ly, Al - to- geth - er love - ly;

Fair - est among ten thou- sand, He's al - to- geth - er love - ly.

WHERE ARE YOU DWELLING?

Emma A. Tiffany.

Geo. C. Hugg.

1. Are you dwelling in the val - ley, The dewless val - ley foul with sin;
2. Are you dwelling on the mountain, The peerless mountain of God's love?
3. Are you in Christ's love a - bid - ing, A - bid-ing in his love each day?

Where the hosts of Sa - tan ral - ly   To keep the Christ from ent'ring in?
Are you drinking from the fountain That's flow-ing free- ly from a - bove?
Are you still the storm out- rid- ing, Still walk- ing in the narrow way?

Then haste thee a- way   from the val- ley, The dewless valley foul with sin,
O dwell ye up- on   the blest mountain, The peerless mountain of God's love;
In Christ's love be ev - er a - bid- ing, A- bide ye in his love each day;

Where the hosts of Sa - tan ral - ly   To keep the Christ from ent'ring in.
  O drink ye from the fountain That's flowing free - ly from a- bove.
The storm still be out - rid- ing, Still walk ye in the narrow way.

140 CALLEST THOU?

HELEN MARION BURNSIDE.

GEO. C. HUGG.

1. Call-est Thou thus, oh Mas - ter? Call-est Thou thus to me?
2. Com-est Thou thus, oh Mas - ter? Com-est Thou thus to me?
3. "Child," said the gracious Mas - ter, With voice di - vine - ly sweet,

Wea-ry and heav - y la - den, Long-ing to come to Thee,
Un-trimm'd, my lamp, and dy-ing, And house not meet for Thee,
I on - ly ask a wel - come; Rest, for my wea - ry feet!

Out in the lone - ly dark - ness Thy dear voice sounds so sweet,
Thou art so great and ho - ly, I am by sin un - done,
Come o'er my low - ly thresh-old, Dark, and de - filed by sin,

ritard.

I am not wor-thy Master, oh no, Not wor-thy to kiss Thy feet.
I am not wor-thy Master, oh no, Not worthy that Thou should'st come.
Tho' all unwor-thy Master, oh come, I pray Thee, come, en-ter in.

FAITHFUL AND TRUE.

Rev. Johnson Oatman, Jr.　　　　　　　　Adam Geibel.

1. I want to be faithful to Je - sus, No matter what path I pur - sue;
2. In face of the foes that op- pose me, By faith I will fight my way through;
3. I've thoughts in my heart I must con-quer, And e - vil desires to sub - due;
4. For on - ly to those who are faith- ful A bright crown is held up to view;

I want to live close to the Sav- iour, I want to be faithful and true.
Since I have been called by the Mas- ter, I want to be faithful and true.
But if I'm to bear his dear im - age, I want to be faithful and true.
So, un - til he calls me to glo - ry, I want to be faithful and true.

CHORUS.

I want to be true to the Mas - ter, I'll do what he bids me to do;

I want to be faithful to Je - sus, I want to be faithful and true.

WITNESSING FOR CHRIST.

DIRDIE BELL.   ADAM GEIBEL.

1. Do you know that Christ is list'ning? Does he hear your accents clear?
2. Once he sought you in his pit - y, You were far out- side the fold;
3. There are oth - ers in the des - ert, Seek them now and tell of him,
4. Does no sound e'er break the stillness? Does he know his child is dumb?

Do you al - ways witness for him, Tell to oth - ers far and near
Oh, his love was deep and ten- der, Have you oft the sto - ry told?
Of his pa - tience and for- bearance When you wandered far from him;
Do not grieve him by your si- lence As the moments go and come!

All the joys of his sal - va- tion, All the rap- ture of his love?
In the wil - der- ness so lone- ly, Je - sus heard your fee- ble cry;
Tell them of the peace and shel- ter Offered to each homeless one;
Thro' the swift- ly fly - ing moments He is list'ning from his throne;

Let him hear your lov - ing utt'rance, He is lean - ing from a - bove!
Brought you home to life and gladness, Do you ev - er tes - ti - fy?
For if you re - fuse to tell them, How can they to Christ be won?
Be a true and faith- ful wit- ness, Speak in eag - er, joy - ous tone.

CHORUS.

Are you wit - ness-ing for Je - sus, Glad to speak a lov - ing word?

List'ning, longing souls surround you, That dear sto - ry have they heard?

UXBRIDGE.

HARRIET AUBER.   LOWELL MASON.

1. Ere mountains reared their forms sublime, Or heav'n and earth in or - der stood ;
2. A thousand a- ges in their flight, With thee are as   a fleet- ing day ;
8. But our brief life's a shadowy dream, A passing tho't, that soon is   o'er,
4. To us, O Lord, the wisdom give Each passing moment so to spend

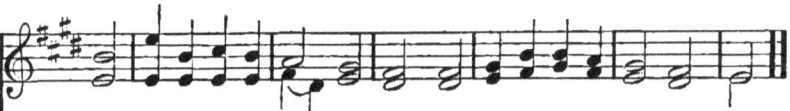

Be- fore the birth of an - cient time, From ev - er- lasting, thou art   God.
Past, present, future to   thy sight At once their various scenes dis - play.
That fades with morning's ear - liest beam, And fills the musing mind no   more.
That we at length with thee may live, Where life and bliss shall nev- er   end.

A. H. A.   A. H. A.

1. O to be there, where the songs of glory Float o'er the waves of the bright crystal sea;
2. O for a voice to proclaim the message In ev-'ry land and the isles of the sea,
3. Now that I've tasted thy love, O Jesus, Tak-en my cross and am following thee,
4. O for a heart that will always love him, Trusting his promise wherev-er I be;

This the refrain of the wondrous sto - ry, "Je - sus has died for me."
"God's on - ly Son is the Friend of sinners, Je - sus has died for me."
Help me to tell this great truth to oth- ers, "Je - sus has died for me."
Bearing in mind this sweet truth so precious, "Je - sus has died for me."

While still I linger in this world be-low, Waiting till homeward I am called to go,
'Tis but a lit-tle that my hands can do For this dear loving One so kind and true,
O that the world would seek the Father's face, Trust in his mercy and forgiving grace;
Washed in the blood of Jesus Christ my King, Thro' endless ages I this song shall sing,

I will repeat o'er and o'er the sto - ry, "Je - sus has died for me."
But I can tell to the world the sto - ry, "Je - sus has died for me."
Then how all hearts would rejoice in singing, "Je - sus has died for me."
"Glo - ry to God, ev - er- last-ing glo - ry, Je - sus has died for me."

A BLESSING FOR ME.

145

E. E. HEWITT.

ADAM GEIBEL.

1. There's a bless-ing for me, When my Saviour I see, On the cross where He
2. There's a bless-ing for me, Grace, a-bund-ant and free, When I bow at the
3. There's a bless-ing for me, When to Je-sus I flee; Ev-'ry bur-den He

died for my sin; There the life-giv-ing tide To my
blood-sprinkled throne; For the Lord will pre-pare Prec-ious
helps me to bear; He will dou-ble my joy, All my

soul is ap-plied, And His Spir-it breaths par-don with-in.
an-swers to pray'r, When I'm trusting His prom-ise a-lone.
foes will de-stroy, 'Till at last, in His glo-ry I share.

CHORUS.

A bless-ing for me, Yes, a bless-ing for me;

Through Je-sus, my Sav-iour, A bless-ing for me.

146 THE JUDGMENT DAY.

REV. JOHNSON OATMAN, JR.

GEO. C. HUGG.

1. At the bar of God you will have to stand, When the books are
2. There you'll meet each friend, there you'll meet each foe, Will they bring you
3. Ev-'ry act of life will be there made known, When we see our
4. Ev-'ry hour we spend in the Master's cause Will be weighed by
5. Let us then live close to the bleeding side Of that precious

opened by the Saviour's hand; Then for ev'ry thought and each word you say
pleasure? will they cause you woe? For the way you act, while on earth you stay,
Saviour on the judgment throne; Many deeds that here we would hide a - way
mercy 'gainst his broken laws; Ev-'ry song we sing, ev- 'ry pray'r we pray,
Saviour, who for us hath died; For if we love him, and his voice o - bey,

CHORUS.

You will have to answer, on the judgment day. ⎫
Will condemn or save you on the judgment day. ⎪
Will be heard by millions, on the judgment day. ⎬ On the judgment day, dreadful
Will be waiting for us on the judgment day. ⎪
Joyfully we'll meet him, on the judgment day. ⎭

judgment day, We shall meet our Saviour on the judgment day; Then what will you do? oh, what will you say When you stand before him on the judgment day?

ALL HAIL THE POWER OF JESUS' NAME.

Rev. E. Perronet. O. Holden.

1. All hail the pow'r of Je- sus' name! Let an - gels prostrate fall;
2. Let ev - 'ry kin- dred, ev - 'ry tribe, On this ter - res- trial ball,
3. Oh, that with yon - der sa- cred throng, We at his feet may fall;

Bring forth the roy- al di - a- dem, And crown him Lord of all;
To him all maj- es - ty ascribe, And crown him Lord of all;
We'll join the ev - er - last- ing song, And crown him Lord of all;

Bring forth the roy- al di - a- dem, And crown him Lord of all.
To him all maj- es - ty ascribe, And crown him Lord of all.
We'll join the ev - er - last-ing song, And crown him Lord of all.

148   I WILL FOLLOW THEE.

IDA L. REED.   ADAM GEIBEL.

1. I will fol-low thee, my Saviour, Tho' the days be dark or bright;
2. I will fol-low thee, my Saviour, Lead me whereso-e'er thou will;
3. I will fol-low thee, my Saviour, Glad, re-joic-ing thus to be

Tho' the path be o-vershadowed, For with thee is joy and light.
Tho' I pass thro' clouds and darkness, Thou wilt be my comfort still.
Walking with thee, hourly, dai-ly, Sharing in thy mer-cy free.

CHORUS.

I will fol-low thee, my Saviour, And I will not fear to keep,

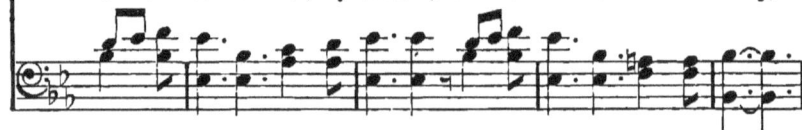

With my hand in thine, the pathway, Tho' the storm-clouds o'er me sweep.

JESUS KNOWS.

149

GEO. C. HUGG.

GEO. C. HUGG.

1. When this poor heart is burdened with grief, No-bod-y knows like Je-sus!
2. When on the mount of joy and de-light, No-bod-y knows like Je-sus!
3. All that I am, or ev-er shall be, No-bod-y knows like Je-sus!

When at the Cross I cry for re-lief, No-bod-y knows like Je-sus!
When faith up-lifts to mansions so bright, No-bod-y knows like Je-sus!
All there remains in glo-ry for me, No-bod-y knows like Je-sus!

CHORUS.

No-bod-y knows like Je-sus! No-bod-y knows like Je-sus!

Precious Re-deem-er, Brother and Friend, No-bod-y knows like Je-sus!

150   AT THE SETTING OF THE SUN.

Rev. Johnson Oatman, Jr.   Geo. C. Hugg.

Not too fast.

1. There is work to do for Je- sus, Work for ev -'ry one   to   do ;
2. Gold - en hours are swift- ly passing, They will nev - er come a- gain ;
3. Men on ev -'ry side are dy- ing, Souls for whom the Saviour died ;

For the fields are white with harvest, But the la - bor- ers are few.
La - bor while the sun is shining, Or you can - not save the grain.
Go and tell them of sal - va-tion, Point them to the Cru - ci- fied.

La - bor for him in life's morning, La - bor till the day is done;
Har- vest time will soon be o - ver, But when life its course has run,
Then when an - gels reap the harvest, When your crown of life is won,

For your toil - ing will be end - ed At the setting of the sun.
Will you have a sheaf for Je - sus At the setting of the sun.
You will stand among the reap- ers At the setting of the sun.

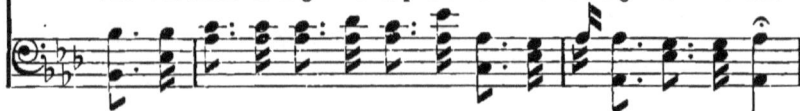

CHORUS.

When your la- - - - bor here is end - ed,
When your la - bor here is end - ed, And your race on earth is run,

And your race...................... on earth is run,
When your la - bor here is end - ed, And your race on earth is run,

Will you have...................... a sheaf for Je - sus
Will you have a sheaf for Je - sus At the set - ting of the sun?

At the set- - - - ting of the sun? Will you
Will you have a sheaf for Je - sus At the setting of the sun? Will you

have........... a sheaf for Je - sus At the setting of the sun?
have a sheaf for Je - sus At the setting of the sun?

AT ANCHOR RIDING.

MRS. HARRIET E. JONES.   GEO. C. HUGG.

1. In the shadow of Thy wings, O dear Re-deemer, I am rest-ing and my
2. In the shadow of Thy wings, O dear Re-deemer, There is blessing both in
3. In the shadow of Thy wings, O dear Re-deemer, There is rapture such as

rest is sweet; When the waves are rising, high I am a - bid - ing, In the
storm and shine; With the wild winds raging fierce, I'm safely hiding In the
none can tell; 'Mid the cares and trials still, my Lord, I'll praise Thee, In the

CHORUS.

shel-ter of this dear re - treat.
shel-ter of the love di - vine.   } Safe, at an-chor rid-ing, in the ha - ven;
shel-ter where I sweetly dwell.

Safe, at an - chor rid - ing, in the ha - ven, Safe, at an - chor

rid - ing in the ha - ven, Bless-ed ha - ven of my Sav-iour's love.

THE LORD NEVER MAKES A MISTAKE. 153

Rev. Johnson Oatman, Jr.   Adam Geibel.

1. When clouds, dark as midnight, hang o-ver my head, When waves of afflic- tion a-
2. If I, like the wand'rer, should walk all a-lone, My couch on the hillside, my
3. If wealth or if honors should take wings and fly, If friends who once flattered should

round me are spread, I know 'tis for my good, so I have no dread,
pil - low a stone, I'll know when the lad - der to heav - en is shown,
then pass me by, Still I will trust Je - sus, and sing till I die,

CHORUS.

The Lord never makes a mistake. The Lord never makes a mistake,

The Lord nev- er makes a mistake; Let him do what he will, I will

trust in him still, The Lord nev - er makes a mis - take.

154 THE KNOCK OF THE NAIL-PIERCED HAND.

JOHN R. CLEMENTS.   JNO. R. SWENEY.

1. Dost thou know at thy bolt - ed heart's-door to-night, The Sav - iour in
2. Out - side he has stood thro' the length of the years, Since Mother the
3. You turn not a- way when a friend's at your door, Here's one there's none
4. All the pain and the shame of his death on the tree A welcome from

meekness doth stand, And longs for admission? pray, lis - ten now To the
love-flame first fanned; You have spurned and rejected, O give heed to-night To the
like in the land, Who asks to come in to for- ev - er a-bide; Heed the
you should command, Since the weight of your sins in his bod - y he bore; Heed the

CHORUS.

knock of the nail-pierced hand. Heed the knock of the nail-pierced hand,
Heed the knock, heed the knock of the nail-pierced hand,

Heed the knock of the nail- pierced hand;...... Swing the door o-pen wide,
Heed the knock, heed the knock of the nail-pierced hand;

Bid him en-ter and abide, Heed the knock of the nail-pierced hand.........
Heed the knock, heed the knock of the nail-pierced hand.

"LOOSE HIM, AND LET HIM GO."

Rev. Johnson Oatman, Jr.   Geo. C. Hugg.

1. When the tempt-er's coils are round thee, Loose him, and let him go;
2. Broth-er cut the cords that bind thee, Loose him, and let him go;
3. Do not be by sa-tan driv-en, Loose him, and let him go;
4. Let him whis-per to you nev-er, Loose him, and' let him go;

When his pres-ence seems to bound thee, Loose him, and let him go.
Bid the tempt-er get be-hind thee, Loose him, and let him go.
Send a fer-vent pray'r to heav-en, Loose him, and let him go.
Would you hap-py be for-ev-er, Loose him, and let him go.

CHORUS.

Loose him, and let him go, Loose him, and let him go;

'Tis the voice of Je-sus say-ing, Loose him, and let him go.

SCATTERING PRECIOUS SEED.

W. A. OGDEN. GEO. C. HUGG.

1. Scat-ter-ing pre-cious seed by the way - side, Scat-ter - ing
2. Scat-ter-ing pre-cious seed for the grow - ing, Scat-ter - ing
3. Scat-ter-ing pre-cious seed, doubt-ing nev - er, Scat-ter - ing

pre-cious seed by the hill - side, Scat-ter - ing pre-cious seed
pre-cious seed, free - ly sow - ing, Scat-ter - ing pre-cious seed
pre-cious seed, trust-ing ev - er, Sow-ing the word with pray'r

o'er the field, wide; Scat-ter-ing pre - cious seed by the way.
trust - ing, know - ing, Sure-ly the Lord will send it the rain.
and en - deav - or, Trusting the Lord for growth and for yield.

CHORUS.

Sow - ing in the morn - - ing, Sow - ing
Sowing the seed, Sowing the precious seed, Sowing the seed,

at the noon - - tide, Sow - ing in the
Sow-ing the pre-cious seed, Sowing the seed,

eve - ning, Sowing the precious seed by the way,
Sowing the precious seed, by the way.

MEAR.

ISAAC WATTS.   A. WILLIAM'S COLL.

1. Sing to the Lord Je - ho-vah's name, And in His strength re-joice;
2. With thanks approach His aw-ful sight, And psalms of hon - or sing;
3. Come, and with hum-ble souls a - dore; Come, kneel be - fore His face:
4. Now is the time, He bends His ear, And waits for your re - quest;

When His sal - va - tion is our theme, Ex - alt - ed be our voice.
The Lord's a God of boundless might, The whole cre - a - tion's King.
Oh, may the crea-tures of His pow'r, Be child-ren of His grace.
Come, lest He rouse His wrath and swear, "Ye shall not see my rest."

WE'LL NEVER TURN BACK ANY MORE.

Rev. Johnson Oatman, Jr.   Geo. C. Hugg.

1. There's a land, we are told, Where the streets are of gold, Just a-
2. There, with palms in their hands, Are the saints from all lands, Singing
3. For our God and the right We have en - tered the fight, And we'll
4. Praise the Lord for his grace, We have en - tered a place Where we're
5. So on God we'll re - ly, Pressing on till we die; Then, when

cross on the bright shining shore;   We've left E - gypt behind
prais - es to God o'er and o'er;   We are marching a- long,
fol - low where he goes be - fore;   For we conquer each day,
safe, tho' the loud tempests roar;   Let the world laugh and sneer,
bat - tles of life all are o'er,   With our Sav-iour we'll rest,
                    shining shore;

That fair coun - try to find, And we'll nev - er turn back an - y more.
Soon we'll join in their song, And we'll nev - er turn back an - y more.
While we fight as we pray, And we'll nev - er turn back an - y more.
We are sat - is - fied here, And we'll nev - er turn back an - y more.
In that land of the blest, And we'll nev - er turn back an - y more.

Chorus.

No, we'll nev - er turn back an - y more,   No, we'll
                                      an - y more,

nev - er turn back an - y more;   We are pressing our way
an - y more;

Toward that fair land of day, And we'll nev- er turn back an - y more.
an- y more.

THATCHER.

Isaac Watts.   Handel.

1. How hon- ored is the place Where we a - dor - ing stand—
2. Bul - warks of grace de - fend The cit - y where we dwell,
3. Lift up th' e - ter - nal gates, The doors wide o - pen fling;
4. Here taste un - min - gled joys, And live in per - fect peace,

Zi - on, the glo - ry of the earth, And beau - ty of the land!
While walls, of strong sal - va - tion made, De - fy th' as- saults of hell.
En- ter, ye na - tions that o - bey The stat - utes of our King.
You that have known Je - hov - ah's name, And ven- tured on his grace.

THE GOSPEL TRAIN.

Rev. Johnson Oatman, Jr.   Geo. C. Hugg.

1. There's a train that runs from the earth to the sky, And
2. There is naught to pay for a ride on this train, For
3. This train makes no noise as it runs thro' the land, For it
4. This train has nev - er been wreck'd on the road, But

ev - 'ry one may ride if they will, It starts from that fountain that
Christ has paid the fare for us all, The poor and the need- y, the
travels on the road-bed of love, Its crew is composed of a
land-ed all her souls in the sky, It can take all the world at a

nev - er runs dry, And it stops on the heav - en - ly hill.
blind and the lame, Can all go, if on Christ they will call.
heav - en - ly band, And its motor pow'r is faith from a - bove.
sin - gle load, Get on board, bid earth's tri - als good - by.

CHORUS.

O sin - ner get on board of the gos - pel train, For it

THE GOSPEL TRAIN. Concluded. 161

runsstraighta-head, nev-er back; It starts on the schedule 'midstthe

wind or the rain, And it nev-er runs off of the track.

HOPE. L. M.

J. NEWTON.   BEETHOVEN.

1. As, when the wea-ry travel-er gains The height of
2. Thus, when the Chris-tian pil-grim views By faith his
3. The thought of heav'n his spir-it cheers, No more he
4. Je-sus, on Thee our hopes we stay, To lead us

some com-mand-ing hill, His heart re-vives, if o'er the
man-sion in the skies, The sight his faint-ing strength re-
grieves for tro-bles past; Nor an-y fu-ture tri-al
on to Thine a-bode; As-sured Thy love will far o'er-

plains He sees his home, tho' dis-tant still.
news, And wings his speed to reach the prize.
fears So he may safe ar-rive at last.
pay The hard-est la-bours of the road. A-MEN.

TRUST IN THE LOVING JESUS.

H. A. T.   Mrs. H. A. Thorn.

1. Trust in the lov-ing Je-sus, Trust him till he comes; Trust him, O faithless wand'rer,
2. Trust in the lov-ing Je-sus, Trust him till he comes; Trust in life's golden morning,

Trust him till he comes. Spread are his wings of healing, Trust him till he comes;
Trust him till he comes. Trust in the glowing noontide, Or night's sa-ble gloom,

CHORUS.

He'll cure thy soul's diseas - es, Trust him till he comes. } Trust ye in Je- sus,
He is thy light and glo-ry, Trust him till he comes. }

Trust him till he comes, Trust ye in Je- sus, Trust him till he comes; Till he

comes,   Till he comes,   Trust ye in Je- sus, Trust him till he comes.
Till he comes,   Till he comes,

THAT LAND BEYOND THE STARS.

Rev. Johnson Oatman, Jr.   Geo. C. Hugg.

1. When the shades of evening gath-er, And the sun has gone to sleep, It is
2. O   I thank the Lord for darkness, For   it makes the stars shine bright, And my
3. Cares of life will soon be o - ver, And the day will soon be done, Then I'll

then I love to lin-ger, While the shadows round me creep, Then I view the
soul is lift - ed upward, When I   see their gold-en light, For I think of
go to that fair country, When my race be- low is run, God will send His

spangled heavens, Sending out their gold-en bars, And in fan - cy I am
that fair country, Where no dis - cord ev - er jars, And I feel home-sick for
an-gels for me, I will get on board their cars, And sweep thro' the golden

car-ried, To that land be-yond the stars, To that land be-yond the stars.
heav-en, For that land be-yond the stars, For that land be-yond the stars.
pathway, To that land be-yond the stars, To that land be-yond the stars.

164 JESUS ALWAYS GOES AHEAD.

REV. JOHNSON OATMAN, JR.   GEO. C. HUGG.

1. Since I made the Lord my choice, Since He made my heart re-joice;
2. Oft, a-cross my path I see, Shad-ows that would fright-en me;
3. In the day or in the night, In the dark or iu the light;
4. When I reach the Jor-dan's brink, Safe with Him I will not shrink;

Ev - 'ry-where that I am led, Je - sus al-ways goes a-head.
But of them I have no dread, Je - sus al-ways goes a-head.
Safe - ly in His steps I tread, Je - sus al-ways goes a-head.
O'er its tide a bridge is spread, Je - sus al-ways goes a-head.

CHORUS.

Praise the Lord I'm, not a-fraid, In dark hours, I'm not dismayed,

For I know where e'er I'm led, Je - sus al-ways goes a-head.

Mrs. Frank A. Breck.   Adam Geibel.

1. Sovereign mer - cy a sin-ner may claim, O tell the sweet message a-
2. Sovereign mer - cy of in - fi - nite worth! 'Tis deep as a fath-om-less
3. Sovereign mer - cy is all I can plead, For I have no good of my

broad; And let us re- joice and give praise to his name, And
sea; As far as "the heavens are high- er than earth," So
own; But God is enough for my ut - ter-most need, And I

CHORUS.

trust in the mer- cy of God. ⎫
great is God's mercy to me. ⎬ Sovereign mercy, a-bundant and free! O
trust in his mer- cy a - lone. ⎭

sovereign mer- cy of God!...... There is mer - cy on high, and

I will re - ly On the sovereign mer - cy of God.

FEAR NOT TO TREAD LIFE'S ROAD.

IDA L. REED.   ADAM GEIBEL.

1. Fear not to tread life's road, dear friend, Tho' dark it sometimes be;
2. Fear not, tho' cares may oft distress, Still hand in hand with thee
3. Fear not, O friend, whate'er may come, Thou canst not be for - got;

God's presence shall thy way at - tend, His love thy light shall be.
Thy Fa - ther walks, to cheer and bless Thy soul in mer - cy free.
With ten - der hand he'll lead thee home, His love will fail thee not.

CHORUS.

Fear not to tread life's changeful way, Where'er the path may trend.

God will be with thee day by day, A nev - er - fail - ing Friend.

SIN NO MORE.

Miriam E. Oatman.   Geo. C. Hugg.

1. When Christ our Saviour was here on earth, And traveled its pathway o'er,
2. Although the Saviour no longer walks And teaches beside the shore,
3. His pleadings heed, then he'll give to thee Joy thou hast ne'er felt be - fore;
4. Tho' while we're here, on this earth be-low, We are tempted o'er and o'er,

He said to a woman, whom he had healed, "Go, daughter, and sin no more."
Yet still he is calling, thro' his dear word, For mortals to sin no more.
If thou wilt but lis-ten to his sweet call, He'll help thee to sin no more.
When up in yon heaven we stand at last With Christ, we will sin no more.

CHORUS.

Sin-ner, the Saviour is call-ing to thee, Call-ing thee o'er and o'er;

"Come, O poor sinner, now come un-to me; Come to me and sin no more."

COMING HOME.

IDA L. REED.
SOLO, OR SOPRANO AND TENOR DUETT.
ADAM GEIBEL.

1. I am com - ing home, dear Saviour, Long I've wan-d'red far from Thee;
2. Long I've been in darkness stray-ing, Now, O Lord, I turn to Thee;
3. Let Thy lov - ing smile, O Sav-iour, Shine a - cross the night of sin;
4. I am com - ing home, my Sav-iour, Wilt Thou take my hand in Thine;

Now I long for peace and par - don, Grant me Thy for-give-ness free.
I am wea - ry of my wand'ring, Hast Thou wel-come still for me?
And its ho - ly rays shall guide me, Gates of right - eou-ness with-in.
Lead me forth from out the dark - ness, By Thy ten - der love di - vine?

CHORUS.

I am com - ing ... Take my soul, ...

I am coming home, dear Saviour, Take my soul, all sin de- filed;

Cleanse its stains, ... O re - ceive ....

Cleanse its stains in Calv'ry's fountain, O receive Thy err-ing child.

OUT OF THE DARKNESS.

169

IDA L. REED.   GEO. C. HUGG.

DUET.

1. Out of the darkness of sor-row and pain, Lead me, my Saviour, my
2. Lead me, my Saviour, I rest in thy care, Give me thy grace all suf-
3. Saviour, I trust in thy pow-er to save, Give me thy strength all life's

spir-it sustain; Let me not fal-ter or faint by the way, Lead me and
fi-cient to bear Ev-'ry temp-ta-tion, each tri-al and wrong, Tender-ly
bat-tles to brave; Out of sin's shadows my soul safe-ly bring, Lead me, O

CHORUS.

guide me from day un-to day. } Lead me, lead me,
guard me life's pathway a-long. }
lead me, my Lord and my King. } Lead me, my Saviour, O pray lead thou me,

Lead me, my Saviour, I trust in thy love; Lead me,
Lead me, my Saviour, I

lead me, Lead me safe homeward to heav-en a-bove.
pray lead thou me,

HAVE YOU FOUND THE PEACE?

Ida L. Reed.   W. F. Fowler.

1. Have you found the peace that passeth un- der - standing? Are you hap- py
2. Have you heard his voice, his gen- tle in - vi - ta - tion? Did you lis - ten
3. O the joy and peace, the deep and boundless mercy, O the blessings

in the Saviour's love? Are your sins washed white in the precious cleansing
to the accents low? Leaving all for him, glad- ly, willing- ly to
he a - lone can give; O the love he bears thee, so blessed, so un-

CHORUS.

fountain? Are you seeking now a home a - bove?
fol- low Wherso - ev - er he hath bid thee go?   O bless- ed peace that
dy- ing, Look to Je- sus, O believe and live.

Je - sus gives, Seek now the price- less treas- ure; Look un - to him and thou shalt live, He'll give thee with- out measure. His wondrous love, his

mer-cies sure, And joys unfad- ing, rich and pure, O look, look and live.

DUNDEE.

J. Addison.   G. Franc.

1. When all thy mer-cies, O my God, My ris - ing soul sur - veys,
2. O how can words with e - qual warmth The grat - i - tude de - clare,
3. When in the slipp'ry paths of youth, With heedless steps I ran,
4. Thro' ev - 'ry pe - riod of my life Thy goodness I'll pur - sue;

Transport - ed with the view, I'm lost In won - der, love, and praise.
That glows with - in my ravished heart? But thou canst read it there.
Thine arm, un - seen, conveyed me safe, And led me up to man.
And af - ter death, in dis - tant worlds, The pleas- ing theme re - new.

172 COVER THEM OVER WITH BEAUTIFUL FLOWERS.

To Miss Florence W. Williams.

REV. JOHNSON OATMAN, JR.   GEO. C. HUGG.

With great feeling.

1. With un - cov - ered head we are standing to - day, Where val - or lies
2. When the trumpet first soun-ded their country's a-larms, They left their dear
3. Sleep on hon-ored dead, e'er remembered you'll be, While ze-phyrs blow
4. Sleep, peace-ful - ly sleep in your dreams, never more Will your rest be
5. In Co-lum - bi - a's Pan-the-on, tem-ple of fame, Your deeds are re -
6. Rest on, un - disturbed by the changes of time, While fin-gers weave

sleep-ing our tri - bute to pay, At the shrine of these dear sainted
fire-sides and sprang to their arms, They fought, bled, and died, to pre -
o - ver the land of the free, Lov-ing hands will e - rect, to your
bro - ken by night-mares of war, Nor re - veil - le call you at
cord - ed, im - mor - tal your name, At re - ci - tal of them base
garlands, your shafts to en - twine, While your graves are refreshed by the

he - roes of ours, And cov - er them o - ver with beau-ti - ful flow'rs.
-serve freedom's bow'rs, Now cov - er them o - ver with beau-ti - ful flow'rs.
mem - o - ry tow'rs, And cov - er you o - ver with beau-ti - ful flow'rs.
still morning hours, Sleep on, cov-ered o - ver with beau-ti - ful flow'rs.
in - fa - my cow'rs, Now rest, cov-ered o - ver with beau-ti - ful flow'rs.
God giv - en show'rs, Rest on, cov-ered o - ver with beau-ti - ful flow'rs.

CHORUS.

O cov - er them o - ver these sol-diers who sleep, They'll not be for -

got - ten, so why should we weep? They saved as a u - nit this

coun-try of ours, So cov - er them o - ver with beau - ti - ful flow'rs.

THE POWER OF LOVE. C. M.

Rev. W. J. Stuart, A. M.   Rev. W. J. Stuart, A. M.

1. How great the pow'r that holds us fast,   To i - dols of the world!
2. How blind are we to all that's good,   When sin obscures the day!
3. But there's a pow'r that's greater still,   Than Sa - tan's or of sins,
4. His grace is free - ly prom-ised those,   Who in His Word be - lieve,
5. Thus stronger is the love that binds   To God's great throne of might,
6. Who would not have this wondrous love,   When its so free - ly giv'n?

How quick the joys of sin are past, Their fol - ly soon un-furl'd!
How weak to do the task we should, When Sa - tan leads the way!
For one who seeks to do God's will, The con - quest sure - ly wins.
They sure - ly con-quer all their foes, New strength they shall re - ceive.
The soul that heaven's wis-dom finds, Will have in - creas-ing light.
Who would not have a home a - bove, At God's right hand in heav'n?

174   WON'T YOU GIVE HIM A TRIAL?

Rev. Johnson Oatman, Jr.   Adam Geibel.

1. O sin - ner, come list to this won - der - ful sto - ry, Much
2. There's on - ly one path - way that reach - es to heav - en, The
3. A home is prepared for the pure and the ho - ly, But

sweeter than ev - er a soul did beguile; Christ Je- sus invites you to
pathway of cross- bearing and self- denial; Now, while Christ invites you, O
naught can there en - ter to mar or de- file; O bring all your sins to the

grace and to glo - ry, O come to him now, won't you give him a trial?
come, be for- giv - en, O come to him now, won't you give him a trial?
meek and the low - ly, O come to him now, won't you give him a trial?

Chorus.

Won't you give him a trial? won't you give him a trial? He'll brighten your pathway and cheer ev - 'ry mile; Come, bask in the sun - light of

his lov- ing smile, O come to him now, won't you give him a trial?

JUST AS I AM.

CHARLOTTE ELLIOT.   WM. B. BRADBURY.

1. Just as I am, with- out   one plea, But that thy blood was shed for me,
2. Just as I am, and wait - ing not To rid my soul of one dark blot,
3. Just as I am, tho' tossed   a-bout With many a   conflict, many a doubt,
4. Just as I am—poor, wretched, blind, Sight, rich- es, healing   of the mind,
5. Just as I am—thou wilt   receive, Wilt welcome, pardon, cleanse, relieve ;
6. Just as I am— thy love unknown Hath brok-en ev- 'ry barrier down ;

And that thou bidd'st me come to thee, O Lamb of God, I come ! I   come !
To thee whose blood can cleanse each spot, O Lamb of God, I come ! I   come !
Fightings within, and fears without, O Lamb of God, I come ! I   come !
Yea, all I need, in thee I find, O Lamb of God, I come ! I   come !
Because thy promise I be- lieve, O Lamb of God, I come ! I   come !
Now, to be thine, yea, thine a- lone, O Lamb of God, I come ! I   come !

"Fear not, for I am with thee."—GEN. 26: 24.

ROY E. MOOAR.   GEO. C. HUGG.

1. We're marching forward brave and strong, We're fighting ever 'gainst the wrong;
2. The sins with-in, and those without, We're pledged to conquer and to rout;
3. Faith is our shield, protecting, true, Hope gives us ev - er strength a-new,

Our watchword grand shall be our song, On, on for Je - sus!
They fall as we our war-cry shout, On, on for Je - sus!
The Love of God will bring us through, On, on for Je - sus!

CHORUS.

On with flying ban-ners! On with glad ho-san - nas! Je - sus Christ is

leading on, Leading on to vic - to - ry, ... Leading on to vic - to - ry.

Ida L. Reed. Geo. C. Hugg.

Fervently.

1. Choose my path, O bless-ed Saviour, Let me, trusting, lean on thee;
2. Let thy wis-dom guide me ev-er, For I dare not trust my own;
3. Life is full of cares perplexing, And a-lone, I lose the way;

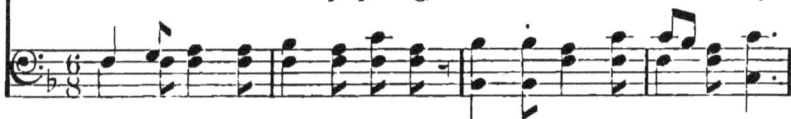

Or-der thou life's joys and du-ties, Just as seemeth good to thee.
Lead thou me in ten-der mer-cy, Leave me not to walk a-lone.
Keep me near to thee, dear Saviour, Choose for me the path, I pray.

CHORUS.

Just as seem-eth good to thee, Just as seem-eth good to thee;

Or-der thou my steps, dear Saviour, Just as seem-eth good to thee.

ENTREAT ME NOT TO LEAVE THEE.

Mrs. Frank A. Breck.   Adam Geibel.

1. How sweet that Bi - ble sto - ry, Of Ruth who left her land
2. "En - treat me not to leave thee, I nev - er can re - turn
3. O sin - ner, leave thy sin - ning, Turn now to Christ the Lord;

To fol - low one who loved the Lord And loved his blest command.
I want the land of prom - ise now, The land of sin I spurn.
Come, seek the cit - y built a - bove, And find a blest re - ward.

She said, "I leave my kin - dred, I seek a path di - vine,
I go, my all for - sak - ing, For I would die with thee;
Like Ruth, of old - en sto - ry, Make Is- rael's God thy stay,

I cast my i - dols all a - way, For Is- rael's God is mine.
'The Lord do so, and more, if aught But death part thee and me.' "
And Christ, the ev - er - last - ing God, Will help thy soul to say,

CHORUS.

"En-treat me not to leave thee, Or turn from following thee,
En-treat me not to leave thee, Hear now my sol - emn vow ;

For where thou go - est, I will go, Thy peo-ple mine shall be. }
I choose thy God to be my God, To be my Sav - iour now. }

SHIRLAND.

H. F. LYTE.   S. STANLEY.

1. My spir - it on thy care, Blest Sav - iour I re - cline ;
2. In thee I place my trust ; On thee I calm - ly rest ;
3. What-e'er e - vents be - tide, Thy will they all per - form ;
4. Let good or ill be - fall, It must be good for me —

Thou wilt not leave me to de - spair, For thou art love di - vine.
I know thee good, I know thee just, And count thy choice the best.
Safe in thy breast my head I hide, Nor fear the com- ing storm.
Se - cure of hav - ing thee in all, Of hav - ing all in thee.

BEAUTIFUL VISION.

Jesse P. Tompkins.

Geo. C. Hugg.

With expression. *Tempo ad lib.*

1. Like a   sil- ver boat the moon glides free, Thro' the soft, white foam of the
2. 'Twas a fan- cy bright, yet fair to me Were the fields of green and the
3. Then a cloud came o'er the sil - ver moon, And a - las, my vis - ion was

star - ry   sea, And my soul seems drift-ing, with rap - id flight, A-
crys - tal sea, And the eyes a - glow with the morning light, With
o'er too soon; If my soul was stirred by that dream so sweet, O

way, far   a- way, on the waves of light; And in thoughtful fan-cy my
nev - er a tear-drop to dim their sight; And the songs that fell on my
what will it be in the morn complete When the bands are broken and

rit.   Chorus.

vision falls On the gates of pearl and the jasper walls. ⎞
list'ning ear Were the sweet home-songs that in dreams I hear. ⎬ Beauti- ful vis - ion,
I am free? Then I'll sail a- way o'er the mystic sea.   ⎠

beau- ti - ful home, Brighter than moon or   stars;.........   O may that
                                        moon or stars;

rit.

vis-ion be true for me, When death shall un-lock the bars..............
unlock the bars.

JESUS, SAVIOUR, PILOT ME.

Rev. Edward Hopper, D. D.

J. E. Gould.

1. Je - sus, Sav - iour, pi - lot me, O - ver life's tempestuous sea,
2. As a moth - er stills her child, Thou canst hush the o- cean wild;
3. When at last I near the shore, And the fear - ful breakers roar

Unknown waves around me roll, Hid-ing rock and treach'rous shoal,
Boist'rous waves o - bey thy will, When thou say- est, "Peace, be still;"
'Twixt me and my peaceful rest, Then while lean-ing on thy breast,

Chart and com - pass come from thee, Je - sus, Sav - iour, pi - lot me.
Wondrous sov'reign of the sea, Je - sus, Sav - iour, pi - lot me.
May I hear thee say to me, "Fear not, I will pi - lot thee."

THE PENTECOSTAL FLAME.

Ida L. Reed.   Geo. C. Hugg.

1. Give us, Lord, thy Ho- ly Spir - it, Let us glo - ri - fy thy name;
2. Loose our tongues, that we may praise thee, That we may to . oth- ers show
3. Souls are seek- ing thy sal - va- tion, We would lead them, Lord, to thee;

Light within our hearts, we pray thee, Now, the pen - te - cost - al flame.
All the sweetness of the bless- ing Thou art wait - ing to be- stow.
Give to us the Spirit's pow - er, Let us each thy witness be.

Chorus.

Come in - to our midst, dear Saviour, Send thy show'rs of blessing down;

Let the full- ness of thy mer - cy All this hour with glo- ry crown.

WHEN THE FIRE CAME DOWN.

Rev. Johnson Oatman, Jr.

Adam Geibel.

1. E - li - jah once stood pray - ing, E - li - jah once stood pray-ing;
2. Great fear fell on the peo - ple, Great fear fell on the peo - ple;
3. I took my sins to Je - sus, I took my sins to Je - sus;
4. For ful - ler con - se - cra - tion, For ful - ler con - se - cra - tion;
5. Great glo - ry fill'd the tem - ple, Great glo - ry fill'd the tem - ple;

That God would send an an - swer, When the fire came down.
They gave to God the glo - ry, When the fire came down.
I laid them on the al - tar, When the fire came down.
Once more I sought the al - tar, When the fire came down.
I caught a sight of heav - en, When the fire came down.

CHORUS.

It fell up - on the al - tar, It fell up - on the al - tar;

Con - sum - ing ev - 'ry por - tion, When the fire came down.

FOR GOD, FOR HOME, AND EVERY LAND.

Dedicated to the W. C. T. U. of America.

REV. JOHNSON OATMAN, JR.   ADAM GEIBEL.

1. To - day all o'er the world one sees, A ban - ner
2. While li - cense rules where Christ-ians dwell, While rum - shops
3. Not with ar - til - lery do we come, Nor scream- ing
4. Not in our fee - ble strength we fight, The Lord of
5. *Faith* tells us we will win the day, *Hope* hov - ers

float - ing on the breeze; Up - on it this in -
send our boys to hell; While Vir - tue trem - bles
fife, nor beat - ing drum; He fights for us who
Hosts will arm the right; But in His bless - ed
o'er us while we pray; *Love* points us with her

crip - tion grand, "For God, and home, and ev - 'ry land."
we will band, "For God, and home, and ev - 'ry land."
has com-mand, "For God, and home, and ev - 'ry laud."
name we stand, "For God, and home, and ev - 'ry land."
gold - en wand, To "God, and home, and ev - 'ry land."

CHORUS.   ban - ner up on high,

O raise the ban - ner up on high, O'er ev - 'ry

FOR GOD, AND HOME, etc. Concluded.

coun - try may it fly;   ev - 'ry where may

coun - try   may it fly; Till all men ev - 'ry

stand,   home and ev - 'ry land.

where may stand, "For God, and home, and   ev - 'ry land."

NAOMI.

ANNIE STEELE.   H. G. NAGELI.

1. Fa - ther what-e'er of   earth-ly bliss Thy sovereign will de - nies,
2. Give me a calm, a   thankful heart, From ev - 'ry mur-mur free;
3. Let the sweet hope that Thou art mine My life and death at - tend;

Ac - cept-ed at Thy throne of grace, Let this pe - ti - tion rise:
The blessings of Thy grace im - part, And make me live to Thee;
Thy presence thro' my journey shine, And crown my journey's end.

ENDUE US WITH POWER.

Ida L. Reed.   Geo. C. Hugg.

1. Come, blessed Saviour, with pentecost-al pow- er, Be thou in our midst to-day ;
2. Come, Jesus, Saviour, in faith we humbly seek thee, Come thou in thy glorious might ;
3. Come, blessed Saviour, thy promis-es ful- fill- ing, Let this be a glorious hour ;

Pour out thy Spir- it a - bundantly this hour, For this do thy children pray.
Come with the gladness and joy of full forgiveness, Each heart fill with joy and light.
Un- to thy children thy Spirit now outpouring, Come thou in thy strength and power.

Chorus.

Come, bless - ed Sav - iour, let thy Ho - ly Spir - it In

pen- te- cost- al fire descend from a - bove ; Pour out thy blessing, en-

due us with power, Power for thy ser- vice, and praise for thy love.

IDA L. REED.   GEO. C. HUGG.

1. Do life's storms a - bove thee roll? Clos - er cling to Je - sus;
2. Are there griefs that bow thee low? Clos - er cling to Je - sus;
3. Are thy days full oft - en drear? Clos - er cling to Je - sus;

There is ref - uge for thy soul, Clos - er cling to Je - sus.
He thine ev - 'ry care doth know, Clos - er cling to Je - sus.
He will give thee joy and cheer, Clos - er cling to Je - sus.

Near - er press - ing to his side, 'Neath his wing se - cure - ly hide,
Do not stand a - part and grieve, At his feet thy bur - den leave;
Trust him, love him, to him cling, Crown him ev - er - more thy King;

Safe - ly in his love a - bide, Clos - er cling to Je - sus.
Ask, and his strong help re - ceive, Clos - er cling to Je - sus.
Glad - ness, peace and rest 'twill bring, Clos - er cling to Je - sus.

THE MUSIC OF HEAVEN.

EMMA A. TIFFANY.   GEO. C. HUGG.

1. O the mu - sic sweet · of heav'n I hear, When glows the ear - ly morn ;
2. O the mu - sic sweet of heav'n I hear, When noontide's with'ring beam
3. O the mu - sic sweet of heav'n I hear, When twi - light shadows fall ;

Its   cadence, fall - ing soft and clear, Awakes the world from sleep.
An - noys and fills my soul with fear,   O priceless then   it seems.
To   dim my faith   no clouds ap- pear, Christ's love o'er- rul - eth   all.

CHORUS.

O the mu - sic sweet of heav'n I hear, It cheers my heart each day ;

O   light- er grows my heav- y load, And brighter shines the way.
the way.

Ida L. Reed.   Geo. C. Hugg.

1. In the full-ness of his mer-cy, Christ my Sav-iour heard my prayer;
2. Thro' my wand'rings still he loved me, Tho' I grieved him oft and sore;
3. Now his peace my heart is fill-ing, Now I'm hap-py all the day;

Stooped to save me, chief of sinners, Tho' I oft refused his care.
Tho' I still his love re-ject-ed, Longed to save me more and more.
Since I've found his full forgiveness, Since my sins are washed a-way.

CHORUS.

In the full-ness of his mer-cy, Ten-der-ly to me he came;

Sought and saved me, wondrous sto-ry, Hal-le-lu-jah to his name.

WHAT IS YOUR HOPE BEYOND?

Rev. Johnson Oatman, Jr.

Geo. C. Hugg.

1. Sin-ner, on life's stormy o - cean, What is your hope be - yond?
2. Mer-cy stands ten-der-ly plead-ing, What is your hope be - yond?
3. Sin-ner, the Saviour is call-ing, What is your hope be - yond?

When ceases this life's com-mo-tion, What is your hope be - yond?
She is for you in-ter-ced-ing, What is your hope be - yond?
Can you not see his blood fall-ing? What is your hope be - yond?

Thoughts of the past keep re-peat-ing, "Life like a shadow is fleet-ing,"
Prayers for your sake are ascend-ing, An-gels a-bove you are bend-ing;
Think of Gethsem-a-ne's gar-den, No longer now your heart hard-en;

Are you prepared for death's greet-ing? What is your hope be - yond?
Think of that life nev-er end-ing, What is your hope be - yond?
In Je-sus Christ there is par-don, What is your hope be - yond?

CHORUS.

Sinner, the moments are fly - ing, Men all around you are dy - ing;

rit.

Soon in the grave you'll be ly - ing, What is your hope be - yond?

HE IS CALLING.

F. W. FABER.

ARRANGED.

1. {There's a wideness in God's mercy, Like the wideness of the sea;
   {There's a kindness in his justice Which is more than (*Omit.*) lib- er- ty.

2. { There is welcome for the sinner, And more graces for the good ;
   { There is mer- cy with the Saviour, There is healing (*Omit.*) in his blood.

He is calling, "Come to me!" Lord, I glad-ly haste to thee.

3 For the love of God is broader
Than the measure of man's mind ;
And the heart of the Eternal
Is most wonderfully kind.

4 If our love were but more simple,
We should take him at his word ;
And our lives would be all sunshine
In the sweetness of our Lord,

192 ACROSS THE BLUE.

Rev. Johnson Oatman, Jr.   Geo. C. Hugg.

1. Beyond the stars our loved ones wait, And watch for us be-side the gate;
2. We long to join our loved ones there, And with them breathe on heaven's air
3. When we shall reach the streets of gold, We will our Saviour's face be-hold;
4. Then let us work and do our best, Soon God will take us home to rest;
5. Till then my soul be still and wait, Soon thou wilt pass the pear-ly gate;

They wait for me, they watch for you, In that fair land a- cross the blue.
The song that is for-ev-er new, In glo-ry land, a- cross the blue.
We'll kiss the hand that led us thro' To mansions fair a- cross the blue.
For if he finds us tried and true, We'll live with him a- cross the blue.
Then what a meet-ing will en-sue With those we love a- cross the blue.

Chorus.

A- cross the blue, a-cross the blue, From Pisgah's height be-hold the view;

Friends wait for me and watch for you, In sin-less land, a-cross the blue.

At a memorial service, held at Chester Heights Camp Meeting, Aug. 2, 1897, a great wave of religious enthusiasm passed over the audience when Rev. C. M. Boswell said, concerning Rev. Wm. Swindells, D. D., "He is away from us to-day, but he is just across the blue awaiting the time for us to come and greet him there. Let us send him word that we will be sure to come."

I'M GOING HOME AT LAST.

I'M GOING HOME AT LAST.

193

Rev. Johnson Oatman, Jr.   Adam Geibel.

1. When I see life's gold-en sun-set lighting up the ros-y West,
2. Tho' the road at times was wea-ry, o-ver which my feet have trod,
3. When I pass down thro' the val-ley and the shad-ow of the dead,

When the shadows backward o'er my way are cast; I shall look up-on that
Tho' thro' man-y trib-u-la-tions I have passed; Yet I soon will reach my
To my blessed Saviour's hand I will hold fast; He has promised to go

moment as the one supreme-ly blest, I'm go-ing home at last.
mansion in the cit-y of our God, I'm go-ing home at last.
with me, so my soul will have no dread, I'm go-ing home at last.

CHORUS.

I'm go-ing home at last,   I'm go-ing home at last; When my
       at last,   at last;

work on earth is end-ed and my race below is run, I'm going home at last.

MY MOTHER'S HANDS.

Mrs. M. E. W.
Slow and with great expression.

Mrs. M. E. Willson.
Sister of the late P. P. Bliss. By per.

1. Oh, those beautiful, beautiful hands! Tho' they neither were white nor small,
2. Oh, those beautiful, beautiful hands! How they cared for my in-fant days!
3. Oh, those beautiful, beautiful hands! As they pressed my ach - ing brow;
4. Oh, those beautiful, beautiful hands! Thin and wrinkled with age they grew;
5. Oh, those beautiful, beautiful hands! I stood by her cof-fin one day,
6. Oh, those beautiful, beautiful hands! I shall clasp them a-gain once more,

Yet my mother's hands were the fair - est, And love-li-est hands of all.
They guided my feet into pleasant paths, And smoothed all the rugged ways.
They cooled the fever and eased the pain, Me-thinks I can feel them now.
But still they toiled on for the child so dear, And her love seemed more tender and true.
And I kissed those hands so cold and white, As qui-et and peaceful she lay.
As my feet touch the bank of the heav'nly land; We shall meet on that shining shore.

CHORUS.

My mother's dear hands, her beautiful hands, Which guided me safe o'er life's sands,

I bless God's name for the mem'ry Of mother's own beau- ti - ful hands.

JESUS NEVER LEAVES THE SHIP.   195

Suggested by the sinking of the steamship Elbe, in the North Sea, Jan, 30th, 1895, in which over 300 lives were lost, and brave Captain Von Goessel *went down with his ship.*

REV. JOHNSON OATMAN, JR.   GEO. C. HUGG.

1. When up-on life's roll-ing o - cean, Fraught with danger is the trip;
2. When the waves are dashing o'er her, Do not fear tho' she may dip;
3. O look up, why are ye fear - ful? Why look down with trembling lip?
4. Oft the ves-sel we must light-en, From all worldly things must strip;
5. Sin - ner come and sail for Heav-en, Have no fears a - bout the trip;

Do not fear 'mid the com-mo - tion,   Je - sus nev - er leaves the ship.
Bet - ter skies yet lie be - fore her,   Je - sus nev - er leaves the ship.
Dry your eyes now sad and tear - ful,   Je - sus nev - er leaves the ship.
Then we'll find as the skies brighten,   Je - sus nev - er leaves the ship.
All on board to Him are giv - en,   Je - sus nev - er leaves the ship.

CHORUS.

Put your trust in your com-man - der,   Not a foot on board shall slip;

In yon port He'll safely land her,   Je - sus nev - er leaves the ship.

"RETURN OF SUMMER."

ALICE JEAN CLEATOR. ROBERT BROOKS FINCH.

Unison. Marcato.

1. We hail thee glorious sum - mer, We welcome thee to - day,
2. We hail thy smile of glad - ness O - Summer fair and sweet;
3. O Summer thou hast brought us A message sweet and fair;

With all thy flow'ry le - gions And all thy song-birds gay.
O let us lay all sad - ness And sigh - ing at thy feet.
O Summer thou hast taught us Of heav - en's brooding care.

The hap-py rills to meet thee With mer - ry laughter run;.............
The woodland ways are ring-ing With many a mer-ry lay;............
Thy gleaming skies of glo - ry Watch o'er the world in love............

While woodland ban-ners greet thee, Be - neath a smiling sun.
Oh let us join in sing - ing With nature's choir to - day.
They tell a glad, sweet sto - ry Of summer lands a - bove.

CHORUS.

We hail thee joy-ous Sum - mer! We welcome thee to - day!

With all thy flow'ry le - gion, And all thy song-birds gay!

BLESSED SAVIOUR.

1. Saviour, blessed Saviour,
   Listen whilst we sing,
   Hearts and voices raising
   Praises to our King.
   All we have we offer,
   All we hope to be,
   Body, soul, and spirit,
   All we yield to Thee.

2. Nearer, ever nearer,
   Christ, we draw to Thee,
   Deep in adoration
   Bending low the knee:
   Thou for our redemption
   Cam'st on earth to die ;
   Thou, that we might follow,
   Hast gone up on high.

3. Great and ever greater
   Are Thy mercies here,
   True and everlasting
   Are the glories there,
   Where no pain, or sorrow,
   Toil, or care, is known,
   Where the angel-legions
   Circle round Thy throne.
   GODFREY THWING.

EVER ONWARD.

1. Brighter still and brighter
   Glows the western sun,
   Shedding all its gladness
   O'er our work that's done.
   Time will soon be over,
   Toil and sorrow past,
   May we, blessed Saviour,
   Find a rest at last.

2. Onward, ever onward,
   Journeying o'er the road
   Worn by saints before us,
   Journeying on to God ;
   Leaving all behind us,
   May we hasten on,
   Backward never looking
   Till the prize is won.

3. Higher then and higher
   Bear the ransomed soul,
   Earthly toils forgotten,
   Saviour, to its goal;
   Where in joys unthought of
   Saints with angels sing,
   Never weary raising
   Praises to their King.
   THWING.

VOICES OF SUMMER.

Ida L. Reed.   Adam Geibel.

Voices in Unison.

1. Car - ol-ing clear   in the   morn - ing sun-light,   Cheer - i - ly
2. O - ver the mead - ows the   honey-bee's humming,   Gath - er their
3. Hail   to the day   to the   chil - dren giv - en,   Glad   with it's

swing-ing on   bough   and spray,   Hear   the glad birds   in their
sweets from the   bloom la - den bowers,   Bright   are the fields   all a -
won - der - ful   mu - sic and light,   Twin - ing our thoughts to our

hap - pi-ness sing-ing,   Greet-ing the dawn of the   Chil - dren's day.
flame with the glo - ry,   Sweet with the per - fume of   beau-ti - ful flowers.
homes   in heav-en,   Draw-ing us near - er that   shore   so bright.

CHORUS.   *Voices in Harmony.*

Cheer - i - ly, cheer - i - ly,   ris - eth the song,   Mer - ri - ly, mer - ri - ly join in the strain, Chil-dren's sweet voi - ces the

e - cho pro-long, Sum-mer's glad mu - sic is sing-ing a - gain.

CROWN HIS HEAD WITH ENDLESS BLESSING.

WILLIAM GOODE.   BEETHOVEN.

1. Crown His head with end - less bless-ing, Who, in God the Father's name,
2. Hail, ye saints, who know His fa - vor, Who with-in His gates are found,
3. Je - sus, Thee our Sav - iour hail - ing; Thee our God in praise we own;
4. Now, ye saints, His pow'r con - fess - ing, In your grate-ful strains a - dore;

With com-pas-sions nev - er ceas - ing, Comes, sal - va - tion to proclaim.
Hail, ye saints, th'exalt - ed Sav - iour; Let His courts with praise a-bound.
High- est hon - ors, nev - er fail - ing, Rise e - ter - nal round Thy throne.
For His mer - cy, nev - er ceas - ing, Flows and flows for ev - er - more.

"OFFERINGS OF LOVE."

ALICE JEAN CLEATOR.　　　　　　　　　J. HOWARD ENTWISLE.

1. Let us bring our off'rings To the Lord to-day; Let us lay them
2. Let us bring our off'rings To the Lord to-day! Oh how great our
3. There are none so hum-ble, There are none so small, But can join the

glad-ly at His feet.　He has led and kept us　All along our way,
blessings from a-bove!　E'en the humblest gift He Will not cast a-way,
ar-my of the King;　Let us hasten glad-ly　To the Lord of all

CHORUS.

And His love is most di-vine-ly sweet. }
If 'tis giv'n in cheer-ful-ness and love! } O how great our mer-cies
Deeds of love and grate-ful-ness to bring! }

from a-bove! O how wondrous is our Saviour's love! Let us haste to

greet Him joy-ful-ly to bring, Gifts of love and ser-vice to the King!

Alice Jean Cleator.   Geo. C. Hugg.

With spirit.

1. O Father lead us Gent-ly by the hand, Through sun and
2. When we would fal - ter Or when we would stray, O Fa- ther,

shad - ow Of the fu - ture - land! Dim and un - trav - el'd
lead us All a - long our way! Help us to ev - er

Lies the way be - fore: O Father, lead us, Lead us ev - er - more!
Clos- er walk to Thee, Thro' ways of darkness Where we can - not see!

CHORUS.

Fears oft af - fright us! Doubt-ings walk be - fore!

ff

O heav'nly Fa - ther lead us, Now, and ev - er - more.

GLORY TO GOD IN THE HIGHEST.

MRS. HARRIET E. JONES.   J. HOWARD ENTWISLE.

1. Now let us sing the song a-gain Heard by the shepherds long a-go; The
2. O sing of Him in joy-ful way, Who first appeared within the stall; O
3. He came to wash a-way our sin, He came to set the cap-tive free, He

joy-ful song, the an-gel strain: Peace and good-will to men be-low.
chant His praise a-loud to-day, He came be-cause He loved us all.
came to gath-er wan-d'rers in, To save and bless us glo-rious-ly.

CHORUS. *Voices in Unison.*

Glo-ry to God in the high-est, Glo-ry to God in the

high-est, Glo-ry to God in the high-est, Sing it, O sing it a-

Voices in Harmony.

gain, Glo-ry to God in the high-est, Peace and good-will to men.

Geo. C. Hugg.   Adam Geibel.

Joyously.

1. Sweet bells ring on your Christmas song, The old, old sto-ry tell-ing, Of
2. Ring "peace on earth, good-will to men," Dear Day-spring of salva-tion; Ring
3. Ring Christ is born, on this sweet morn, A babe in low-ly manger; While
4. Ring out sal-va-tion full and free, To ev-'ry clime and nation, Ring

an - gels bright on plains of light, And heav'nly cho - rus swell-ing.
near and far, o'er moor and fen, Ring joy to ev - 'ry na - tion.
an - gel throng, with song up-borne, Pro-claim the new-born Stran-ger.
out the news to land and sea, Glad tid-ings of sal - va - tion.

CHORUS.

Ring on,...... ring on,...... ye bless-ed Christmas bells ring on, Spread
ring on,   ring on,

forth the news that Christ is born On this sweet Christmas morn.

THE BLESSED STORY.

ADAM GEIBEL.   ADAM GEIBEL.

1. Sing, O sing the bless - ed sto - ry, Christ the Lord is
2. Sing, O sing the bless - ed sto - ry, Christ the Lord is
3. Sing, O sing the bless - ed sto - ry, Christ the Lord is
4. Sing, O sing the bless - ed sto - ry, Christ the Lord is

born in glo - ry: Christ - mas morn dark night dis - pels,
born in glo - ry: We our glad ho - san - nas sing,
born in glo - ry: Born His peo - ple to re - deem,
born in glo - ry: Now is man from sin set free,

CHORUS.

Ring o'er all the world the bells.
Let the bells a cho - rus ring.
Ring ye bells the glo - rious theme.   } Ring,   ring,
Ring ye bells o'er land and sea.

Ring, ring, ring, ring,

hap - py Christmas bells, O'er all the world your mu - sic swells;

ring, ring, ring, O'er all the world your mu - sic swells; Ring,

Ring, ring on this bless-ed morn, For Christ the Lord is

ring, ring, ring, ring, ring, ring, ring, For

born............ Sing, sing, glo - ry be to God, On

Sing, sing, sing, sing, sing, sing, sing, On

earth good - will and peace to men: Glo - ry be to

earth good - will and peace to men. Sing

God on high, Christ is born in Beth - le - hem.

CHRIST IS BORN IN BETHLEHEM.

CHARLES WESLEY.   GEO. C. HUGG.

1. Hark! the her - ald an - gels sing: Glo-ry to the new - born
2. Christ, by high - est heav'n a - dored; Christ, the ev - er - last - ing
3. Hail, the heav'n-born Prince of Peace, Hail, the Sun of Right - eous-

King;...... Peace on earth and mer - cy mild,
Lord;...... Late in time be - hold Him come,
ness!....... Light and life to all He brings,

God and sin - ners rec - on - ciled! Joy - ful all ye
Off - spring of the Vir - gin's womb, Veiled in flesh the
Ris'n with heal - ing in His wings. Mild He lays His

na - tions rise, Join the tri - umph of the skies;.....
God - head see; Hail th' in - car - nate De - i - ty:........
glo - ry by, Born that man no more may die:........

With th' angel - ic host pro-claim, Christ is born in Beth - le - hem.
Pleased as Man with men to dwell; Je - sus our Emman - u - el!
Born to raise the sons of earth, Born to give them sec - ond birth.

CHORUS.

O Beth - le - hem, dear Beth - le - hem, Hark how the glad notes ring!

Ho - san - na in the high - est, Ex - alt the new-born King!

The an - gel throng His praise pro-long, Glo - ry to God they sing,

While heav'n and earth proclaim the birth Of Christ, the new-born King!

208

O LOVELY STAR.

Adam Geibel.
DUETT.

Adam Geibel.

1. O love-ly star in heav'n so bright, That guides the shepherds thro' the
2. O love-ly star, di-rect our feet, That we may haste our Lord to
3. O Star di-vine il-lume our way, That we may gain e-ter-nal

night To where the bless - ed Sav-iour lay, In Bethlehem's
greet; And gath - er 'round like Ma - gi old, Or shepherds,
day, And live while end - less a - ges roll, Safe shel-tered

man - ger far a - way.
hast - 'ning from the fold.
in Thy heav'nly fold.

CHORUS.

O Star di - vine, shed on us

here Thy beams of love and Christmas cheer, And an - gels

sing the song a - gain Of peace on earth, good - will to men.

IDA L. REED.   J. HOWARD ENTWISLE.

Cheerfully.

1. Hark the bells, I hear them chiming, Clear and sweet o'er sea and land,
2. Un - to earth is born a Saviour, Now methinks I hear the strain,
3. Hap - py bells, I love to hear them, Ringing out the old, sweet song,

Once a - gain the angel's message, May it reach to ev - 'ry land.
As the sil - ver tones are ringing, Mer - ri - ly the glad refrain.
Glo - ry in the high-est, glo - ry, Let all tongues the strain prolong.

CHORUS.   *rit.*

Peace, good-will, the bells are chiming, Hark the mu - sic soft and low,

Peal - ing out the old, sweet sto - ry, As they're swinging to and fro.

210

HAIL THE GLAD DAY.

REV. JOHNSON OATMAN, JR.   ADAM GEIBEL.

1. The buds and flow'rs to life are wak-ing, And for-est songsters
2. Each heart to-day with joy is beam-ing, The air is fill'd with
3. As flow'rs and buds were seen ap-pear-ing, Up-on the rod of
4. To-day as round the tomb we lin-ger, We find our *faith* grows

sing - ing, While child - ren bright, all gloom for - sak - ing, Send
glad - ness, While peace and love their rays are streaming, Dis -
An - ron, So from the tomb, all a - ges cheer-ing, Ap -
bright - er, *Hope* points the way with in - dex fin - ger, While

forth their car - ols ring - ing! All glo - ry to the
pell - ing thoughts of sad - ness, The earth from sleep now
peared the rose of Sha - ron, Think of One flower to
Love makes du - ty light - er, When with the last great

Lamb we ren - der, The Prince of Life and glo - ry;
wakes in beau - ty, Ar - rayed in spring-garb ver - nal,
Mor - tals giv - en, When earth her for - ces ral - ly,
foe we've striv - en, We shall not sleep for - ev - er,

We praise His name in strains so ten-der, And her-ald the old sto - ry.
Re - mind-ing us that aft - er du - ty, Our joys shall be e - ter - nal.
The fair - est flow'r in earth or heav-en, The Lil - y of the Val - ley.
But rise to live with Christ in heav-en, Where death will enter nev - er.

CHORUS. *Voices in unison.*

Christ now is ris - - en, Might - y to
Shout, shout the tid - ings, O'er land and

save!............. Burst is the pris - on, And
sea!............. Je - sus is ris - en! And

Voices in harmony.

con - quered the grave!......... man now is free.

HE AROSE.

Geo. C. Hugg.

Geo. C. Hugg.

Slowly.

1. Low - ly entombed He lay, My bless - ed Sav - iour;
2. Vain - ly they watch Him, now, My bless - ed Sav - iour;
3. Burst - ing the seal, He rose, My bless - ed Sav - iour;

Wait - ing the prom - ised day, My prec - ious Lord.
Sure - ly He 'll keep His vow, My prec - ious Lord.
Scatter-ing His arm - ed foes, My prec - ious Lord.

Chorus. *faster.*

Up from the tomb He a-rose! And in triumph, vanquish'd all His
He a-rose!

foes, . . He a-rose a victor o'er the realms of night; And He reigns forever with His
all His foes,

saints in light, He a-rose, He a - rose, Victor o-ver all His foes.
He arose, He arose,

EASTER BELLS.

213

Rev. Johnson Oatman, Jr.   Florence W. Williams.

1. Loud-ly, loud-ly, East - er bells are ring - ing, Glad-ly, glad-ly, hap - py
2. Praise Him, praise Him, while the bells are ring - ing, Glo - ry, glo - ry, may each
3. Once more, once more, set the bells to ring - ing, Loud-er, loud- er, may each

voic- es sing- ing, Christ the Lord is ris - en, From His gloom-y pris - on,
heart keep sing-ing, Tho' the grave in-fold Him, Yet it could not hold Him,
voice keep sing-ing, Swell the bless-ed sto - ry, Je - sus lives in glo - ry,

Glo - ry to His ho - ly name; Ring - ing, ring - ing, keep the
Laud and mag - ni - fy His name; Hark - en, hark - en, clear the
Bless - ed be His ho - ly name; Praise Him, praise Him, while the

joy bells ring-ing, Glad-ly, glad-ly, voic- es join in sing - ing, Bless-ed
bells are ring-ing, Join them, join them, hearts and voices sing - ing, To the
bells are ring-ing, Glad news, glad news, ev - 'ry where keep singing, Heav-en's

tribute bringing, Upward songs are winging, On this hap-py East- er day.
Saviour clinging, Now with joy up-springing, Praise Him on this East- er day.
gates are swing-ing, An- gels join in sing- ing, Prais-es on this East- er day.

ONCE MORE WE ASSEMBLE.

REV. JOHNSON OATMAN, JR.   ROBT. BROOKS FINCH.

1. Once more we as - sem - ble At this Eas - ter time,
2. Soft the winds are blow - ing O - ver hill and dale,
3. 'Twas up - on the Eas - ter That our Lord a - rose,
4. Let us learn the les - sons Of the Eas - ter - tide,

While the birds are sing - ing, And the sweet bells chime.
While the flow'rs are bloom-ing Sweet-ly in the vale.
Com - ing forth tri - um - phant O - ver all His foes.
Let us spread its bless - ings Ev - er far and wide.

Once a - gain has spring - time Come our hearts to cheer,
From the death of win - ter Earth a - wakes once more,
While the fiends of dark - ness Back-ward then were hurled,
For as rose the Sav - iour We shall al - so rise,

Ped.

Bring-ing with it Eas - ter, Best day of the year.
Now each day ap - pear - ing Brigh-ter than be - fore.
Rose to shed His glo - ry O'er a sin - cursed world.
And if we are faith - ful Dwell in Par - a - dise.

215

ONCE MORE WE ASSEMBLE. Concluded.

CHORUS.

Set the bells to ring - ing, Sweet-ly let them chime,

May each heart be hap - py, At this Eas - ter time.

HARK, THE BELLS ARE RINGING.

IDA L. REED.   GEO. C. HUGG.

Bells.

1. Hark, the bells are ring - ing, Sweet and low,
2. Call - ing to the wan - d'rers, Far and wide,
3. Ring the bless - ed tid - ings, Glad - ly ring,

In the stee - ples swing - ing, To and fro.
Tell - ing how for sin - ners Je - sus died.
O - ver earth He reign - eth Prince and King.

HARK, THE BELLS ARE RINGING. Concluded.

Tell - ing the old sto - ry, How He died for men,
O the bless - ed sto - ry, Ring it loud and clear,
All shall bow be - fore Him, And His might pro - claim,

Christ the King of Glo - ry, Now He lives a - gain.
Bells of Eas - ter chime it, Till all na - tions hear.
King of kings is Je - sus, Bless - ed be His name.

CHORUS.

Ring-ing, ring-ing, Sweet and low, Swinging, swinging, To and fro.

Clear and sweet the mu-sic swells, O'er the hills and down the dells,

Christ our Sav-iour lives a-gain, King of kings o'er earth to reign.

BOYLSTON. S. M.—Key C.

A charge to keep I have,
A God to glorify;
A never-dying soul to save,
And fit it for the sky.

2 To serve the present age,
My calling to fulfill,—
O may it all my powers engage,
To do my Master's will.

3 Help me to watch and pray,
And on thyself rely,
Assured, if I my trust betray,
I shall forever die.
—Charles Wesley.

LABAN. S. M.—Key C.

My soul, be on thy guard;
Ten thousand foes arise;
And hosts of sin are pressing hard
To draw thee from the skies.

2 O watch, and fight, and pray,
The battle ne'er give o'er;
Renew it boldly ev'ry day,
And help divine implore.

3 Fight on, my soul, till death
Shall bring thee to thy God;
He'll take thee at thy parting breath,
Up to his blest abode.
—Geo. Heath.

BETHANY.—Key G.

Nearer, my God, to thee!
Nearer to thee,
E'en though it be a cross
That raiseth me;
Still all my song shall be,
"Nearer, my God, to thee,
Nearer to thee!"

2 Though like a wanderer,
The sun gone down,
Darkness be over me,
My rest a stone,
Yet in my dreams I'd be
Nearer, my God, to thee,
Nearer to thee!

3 There let my way appear,
Steps unto heaven;
All that thou sendest me,
In mercy given;
Angels to beckon me
Nearer, my God, to thee,
Nearer to thee!
—Mrs. S. F. Adams.

HOLY GHOST, WITH LIGHT DI-VINE.—Martin, Key F.

Holy Ghost, with light divine,
Shine upon this heart of mine;
Chase the shades of night away,
Turn my darkness into day.

2 Holy Ghost, with power divine,
Cleanse this guilty heart of mine;
Long hath sin, without control,
Held dominion o'er my soul.

3 Holy Ghost, with joy divine,
Cheer this saddened heart of mine;
Bid my many woes depart,
Heal my wounded, bleeding heart.

4 Holy Spirit, all divine,
Dwell within this heart of mine;
Cast down ev'ry idol-throne,
Reign supreme—and reign alone.
—A. Reed.

MARCHING TO ZION.—Key G.

Come, ye that love the Lord,
And let your joys be known;
‖: Join in a song with sweet accord, :‖
‖: And thus surround the throne. :‖

CHO.—We're marching to Zion,
Beautiful, beautiful Zion;
We're marching upward to Zion,
The beautiful city of God.

2 Let those refuse to sing
Who never knew our God,
‖: But children of our heavenly King :‖
‖: May speak their joys abroad. :‖

3 The hill of Zion yields
A thousand sacred sweets,
‖: Before we reach the heavenly fields, :‖
‖: Or walk the golden streets. :‖ ·
—Isaac Watts.

WORK.—Key F.

Work, for the night is coming,
Work through the morning hours;
Work, while the dew is sparkling,
Work 'mid springing flowers;
Work, when the day grows brighter,
Work, in the glowing sun;
Work, for the night is coming,
When man's work is done.

2 Work, for the night is coming,
Work through the sunny noon;
Fill brightest hours with labor,
Rest comes sure and soon.
Give every flying minute
Something to keep in store;
Work, for the night is coming,
When man works no more.
—Annie Walker.

COME TO JESUS.—Key G.

Come to Jesus, come to Jesus !
2 He will save you! 10 He'll forgive you.
3 Oh, believe him! 11 Flee to Jesus !
4 He is able. 12 He will cleanse you.
5 He is willing. 13 He will clothe you.
6 He'll receive you 14 Jesus loves you.
7 Call upon him ! 15 Don't reject him !
8 He will hear you. 16 Only trust him !
9 Look unto him ! 17 Hallelujah, Amen !

ROCK OF AGES.—Key B♭.

Rock of Ages, cleft for me,
Let me hide myself in thee ;
Let the water and the blood,
From thy wounded side which flowed,
Be of sin a double cure,
Save from wrath and make me pure.
2 Could my tears forever flow,
Could my zeal no languor know,
This for sin could not atone—
Thou must save, and thou alone ;
In my hand no price I bring,
Simply to thy cross I cling.   —Toplady.

HOLY SPIRIT.—Key G.

Holy Spirit, faithful guide,
Ever near the Christian's side,
Gently lead us by the hand,
Pilgrims in a desert land ;
Weary souls for e'er rejoice,
While they hear that sweetest voice
Whispering softly, "Wanderer, come !
Follow me, I'll guide thee home."
2 Ever-present, truest friend,
Ever near thine aid to lend,
Leave us not to doubt and fear,
Groping on in darkness drear ;
When the storms are raging sore,
Hearts grow faint, and hopes give o'er,
Whisper softly, "Wanderer, come !
Follow me, I'll guide thee home."
—M. M. Wells.

LORD'S PROTECTION.—Hebron,
L. M., Key B♭.

Thus far the Lord hath led me on,
Thus far his power prolonged my days;
And every evening shall make known
Some fresh memorial of his grace.
2 Much of my time has run to waste,
And I, perhaps, am near my home ;
But he forgives my follies past,
He gives me strength for days to come.
3 I lay my body down to sleep ;
Peace is the pillow for my head,
While well appointed angels keep
Their watchful stations round my bed.
4 Thus, when the night of death shall come,
My flesh shall rest beneath the ground,
And wait thy voice to break my tomb,
With sweet salvation in the sound.
—Isaac Watts.

SWEET HOUR.—Key D.

Sweet hour of prayer, sweet hour of prayer,
That calls me from a world of care,
And bids me, at my Father's throne,
Make all my wants and wishes known !
In seasons of distress and grief,
My soul has often found relief,
And oft escaped the tempter's snare,
By thy return, sweet hour of prayer.
2 Sweet hour of prayer, sweet hour of prayer,
May I thy consolation share,
Till, from Mount Pisgah's lofty height,
I view my home, and take my flight !
This robe of flesh I'll drop, and rise
To seize the everlasting prize ;
And shout, while passing through the air,
Farewell, farewell, sweet hour of prayer !
—W. W. Walford.

THE CHILD OF A KING.—Key F.

My Father is rich
   In houses and lands,
He holdeth the wealth
   Of the world in his hands !
Of rubies and diamonds,
   Of silver and gold,
His coffers are full,
   He has riches untold !
CHO.—I'm the child of a King !
   The child of a King !
With Jesus, my Saviour,
   I'm the child of a King.
2 A tent or a cottage,
   Why should I care?
They're building a palace
   For me over there.
Though exiled from home,
   Yet still I may sing :
"All glory to God,
   I'm the child of a King."
—H. E. Buell.

WEBB.—Key B♭.

Stand up, stand up for Jesus,
   Ye soldiers of the cross ;
Lift high his royal banner,
   It must not suffer loss :
From victory unto victory
   His army shall he lead,
Till every foe is vanquished
   And Christ is Lord indeed.
2 Stand up, stand up for Jesus,
   The trumpet call obey ;
Forth to the mighty conflict,
   In this his glorious day :
"Ye that are men, now serve him,"
   Against unnumbered foes ;
Your courage rise with danger,
   And strength to strength oppose.
—Geo. Duffield, Jr.

SILVER ST.—Key C.

Grace ! 'tis a charming sound,
Harmonious to the ear ;
Heaven with the echo shall resound,
And all the earth shall hear.

2 Grace first contrived a way
To save rebellious man ;
And all the steps that grace display,
Which drew the wondrous plan.

3 Grace taught my roving feet
To tread the heavenly road ;
And new supplies each hour I meet,
While pressing on to God.

4 Grace all the work shall crown
Through everlasting days ;
It lays in heaven the topmost stone,
And well deserves our praise.
—Philip Doddridge.

COME, HOLY SPIRIT.

Come, Holy Spirit, calm my mind,
And fit me to approach my God ;
Remove each vain, each worldly thought,
And lead me to the blest abode.

2 Hast thou imparted to my soul
A living spark of holy fire?
Oh ! kindle now the sacred flame,
Make me to burn with pure desire.

3 A brighter faith and hope impart,
And let me now my Saviour see ;
Oh ! soothe and cheer my burdened heart
And bid my spirit rest in thee.

HE LEADETH ME.—Key D.

He leadeth me ! O blessed thought !
O words with heavenly comfort fraught !
Whate'er I do, where'er I be,
Still 'tis God's hand that leadeth me.

Cho.—He leadeth me, he leadeth me,
By his own hand he leadeth me ;
His faithful follower I would be,
For by his hand he leadeth me.

CLEANSING FOUNTAIN.—Key C.

There is a fountain filled with blood
Drawn from Immanuel's veins ;
And sinners, plunged beneath that flood,
Lose all their guilty stains.

2 The dying thief rejoiced to see
That fountain in his day ;
And there may I, though vile as he,
Wash all my sins away.

3 Thou dying Lamb ! thy precious blood
Shall never lose its power
Till all the ransomed Church of God
Are saved, to sin no more.
—Wm. Cowper.

THE SOLID ROCK.—Key G.

My hope is built on nothing less
Than Jesus' blood and righteousness ;
I dare not trust the sweetest frame,
But wholly lean on Jesus' name :
On Christ, the solid rock, I stand ;
‖ : All other ground is sinking sand. :‖

2 When darkness seems to veil his face,
I rest on his unchanging grace ;
In every high and stormy gale,
My anchor holds within the veil :
On Christ, the solid rock, I stand ;
‖ : All other ground is sinking sand. :‖
—Edward Mote.

MAITLAND.—Key Bb.

Must Jesus bear the cross alone,
And all the world go free?
No ; there's a cross for ev'ry one,
And there's a cross for me.

2 The consecrated cross I'll bear
Till death shall set me free ;
And then go home my crown to wear,
For there's a crown for me.

3 O precious cross ! O glorious crown !
O resurrection day !
Ye angels from the stars come down,
And bear my soul away.
—G. N. Allen.

DUNDEE.—Key Eb.

Come, Holy Spirit, heav'nly Dove,
With all thy quick'ning powers ;
Kindle a flame of sacred love
In these cold hearts of ours.

2 Father, and shall we ever live
At this poor dying rate—
Our love so faint, so cold to thee,
And thine to us so great ?

3 Come, Holy Spirit, heav'nly Dove,
With all thy quick'ning powers ;
Come, shed abroad a Saviour's love,
And that shall kindle ours.
—Isaac Watts.

DENNIS.—Key F.

Blest be the tie that binds
Our hearts in Christian love ;
The fellowship of kindred minds
Is like to that above.

2 Before our Father's throne,
We pour our ardent prayers ;
Our fears, our hopes, our aims are one,
Our comforts, and our cares.

3 We share our mutual woes,
Our mutual burdens bear ;
And often for each other flows
The sympathizing tear.

4 When we asunder part,
It gives us inward pain ;
But we shall still be joined in heart,
And hope to meet again.
—John Fawcett.

LENNOX.—Key B♭.

Arise, my soul, arise,
Shake off thy guilty fears ;
The bleeding Sacrifice
In my behalf appears :
Before the throne my Surety stands
My name is written on his hands.

2 He ever lives above,
For me to intercede ;
His all-redeeming love,
His precious blood to plead :
His blood atoned for all our race,
And sprinkles now the throne of grace.

3 Five bleeding wounds he bears,
Received on Calvary ;
They pour effectual prayers,
They strongly plead for me :
"Forgive him, O forgive," they cry,
"Nor let that ransomed sinner die."

4 My God is reconciled ;
His pardoning voice I hear ;
He owns me for his child ;
I can no longer fear :
With confidence I now draw nigh,
And, "Father, Abba, Father," cry.
—Charles Wesley.

RATHBUN.—Key C.

In the cross of Christ I glory,
Tow'ring o'er the wrecks of time ;
All the light of sacred story
Gathers round its head sublime.

2 When the woes of life o'ertake me,
Hopes deceive and fears annoy,
Never shall the cross forsake me—
Lo ! it glows with peace and joy.

3 Bane and blessing, pain and pleasure,
By the cross are sanctified ;
Peace is there, that knows no measure,
Joys that through all time abide.
—John Bowring.

EVAN.—Key A♭.

Forever here my rest shall be,
Close to thy bleeding side ;
This all my hope and all my plea—
For me the Saviour died.

Cho.—‖: Blessed be the name, :‖
Blessed be the name of the Lord ;
‖: Blessed be the name, :‖
Blessed be the name of the Lord.

2 My dying Saviour and my God,
Fountain for guilt and sin,
Sprinkle me ever with thy blood,
And cleanse and keep me clean.

3 Wash me, and make me thus thine own;
Wash me, and mine thou art ;
Wash me, but not my feet alone,—
My hands, my head, my heart.

4 Th' atonement of thy blood apply,
Till faith to sight improve ;
Till hope in full fruition die,
And all my soul be love.
—Charles Wesley.

AMERICA.—Key F.

My country ! 'tis of thee,
Sweet land of liberty,
Of thee I sing :
Land where my fathers died !
Land of the pilgrims' pride !
From every mountain side
Let freedom ring !

2 My native country, thee,
Land of the noble, free,
Thy name I love ;
I love thy rocks and rills,
Thy woods and templed hills :
My heart with rapture thrills
Like that above.

3 Let music swell the breeze,
And ring from all the trees
Sweet freedom's song :
Let mortal tongues awake ;
Let all that breathe partake ;
Let rocks their silence break,
The sound prolong.

4 Our fathers' God ! to thee,
Author of liberty,
To thee we sing :
Long may our land be bright
With freedom's holy light ;
Protect us by thy might,
Great God, our King !
—S. F. Smith.

MARTYN.—Key F.

Jesus, Lover of my soul,
Let me to thy bosom fly,
While the nearer waters roll,
While the tempest still is high !
Hide me, O my Saviour, hide,
Till the storm of life is past ;
Safe into the haven guide,
O receive my soul at last !

2 Other refuge have I none ;
Hangs my helpless soul on thee :
Leave, O leave me not alone,
Still support and comfort me :
All my trust on thee is stayed,
All my help from thee I bring ;
Cover my defenceless head
With the shadow of thy wing !

3 Thou, O Christ, art all I want ;
More than all in thee I find ;
Raise the fallen, cheer the faint,
Heal the sick, and lead the blind.
Just and holy is thy name,
I am all unrighteousness :
Vile and full of sin I am,
Thou art full of truth and grace.
—Charles Wesley.

INDEX OF TITLES.

221

INDEX OF FIRST LINES.

224   INDEX OF FIRST LINES.

INDEX OF SUBJECTS.